AF255739

QUARANTINIS
on the Balcony

WRITTEN AND PHOTOGRAPHED BY **MICHELLE FRANKLIN**

For Baron

THANK YOU

To my friends and family that listened to my ideas, liked my Instagram and Facebook posts every day, and supported me through this project – I sincerely appreciate it! Thanks to Tara, Deena, Art, Tracy and Steve for drinking every cocktail – even the ones that failed. A special thank you to my dad for inspiring me to write this and constantly encouraging me along the way.

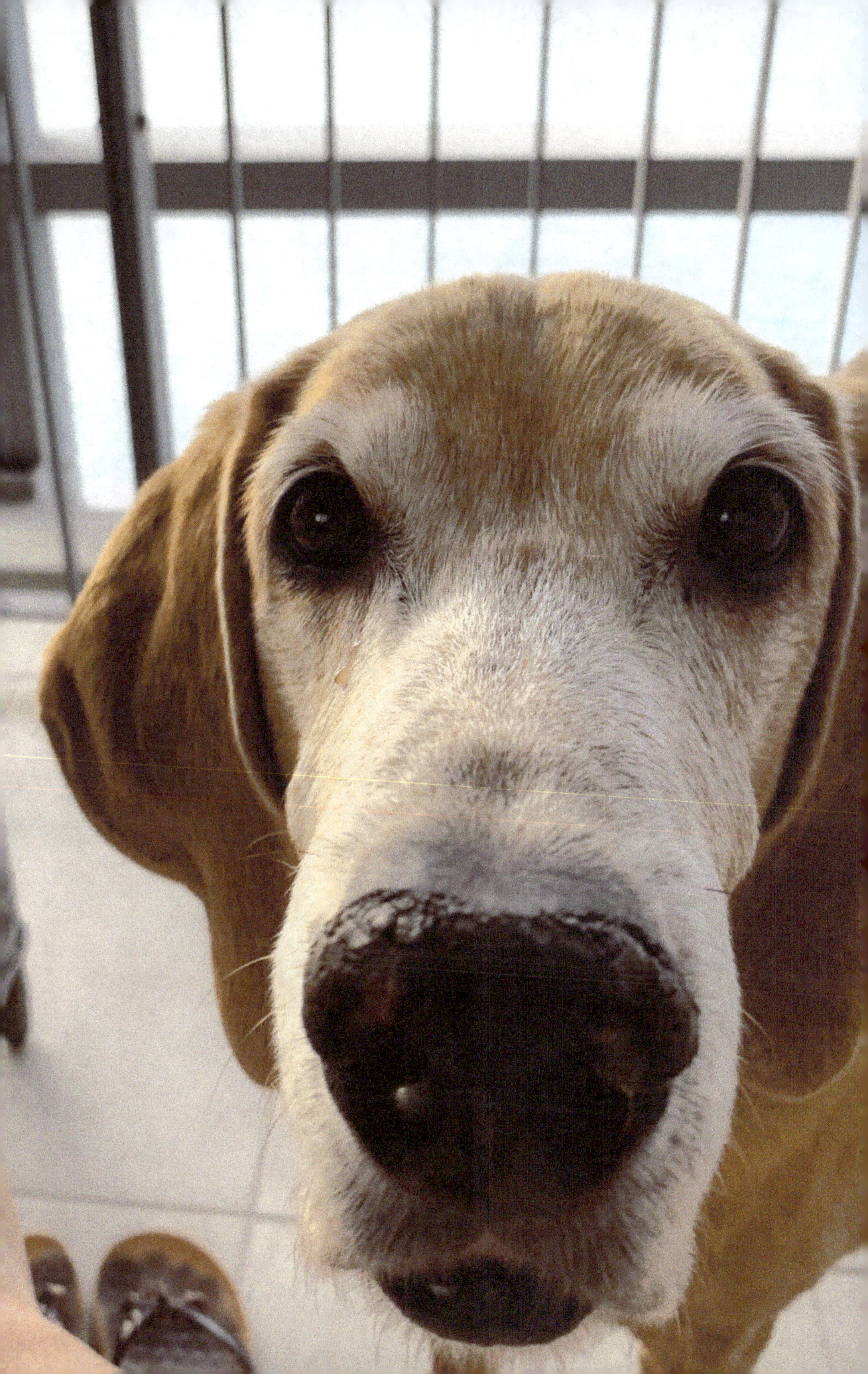

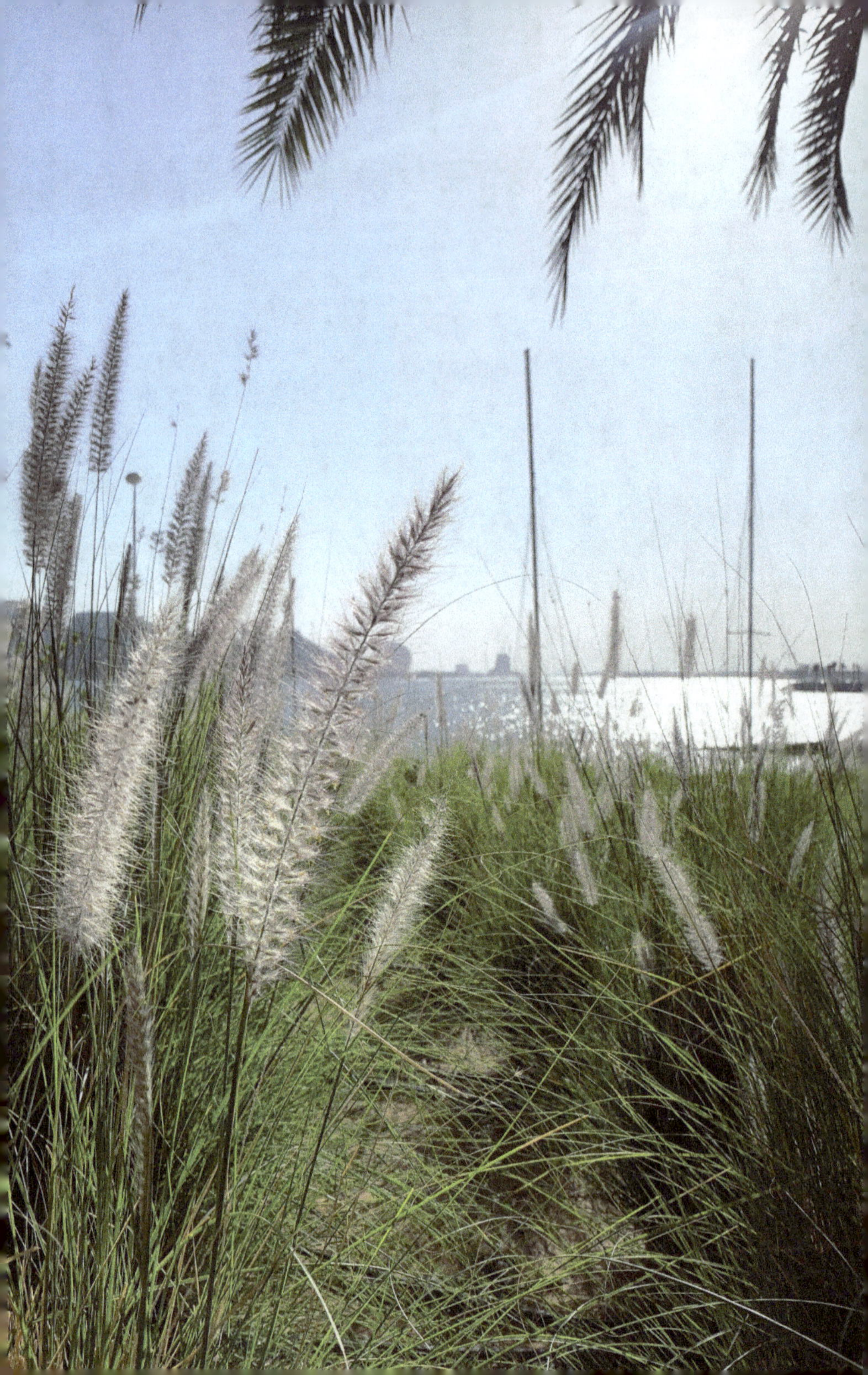

CONTENTS

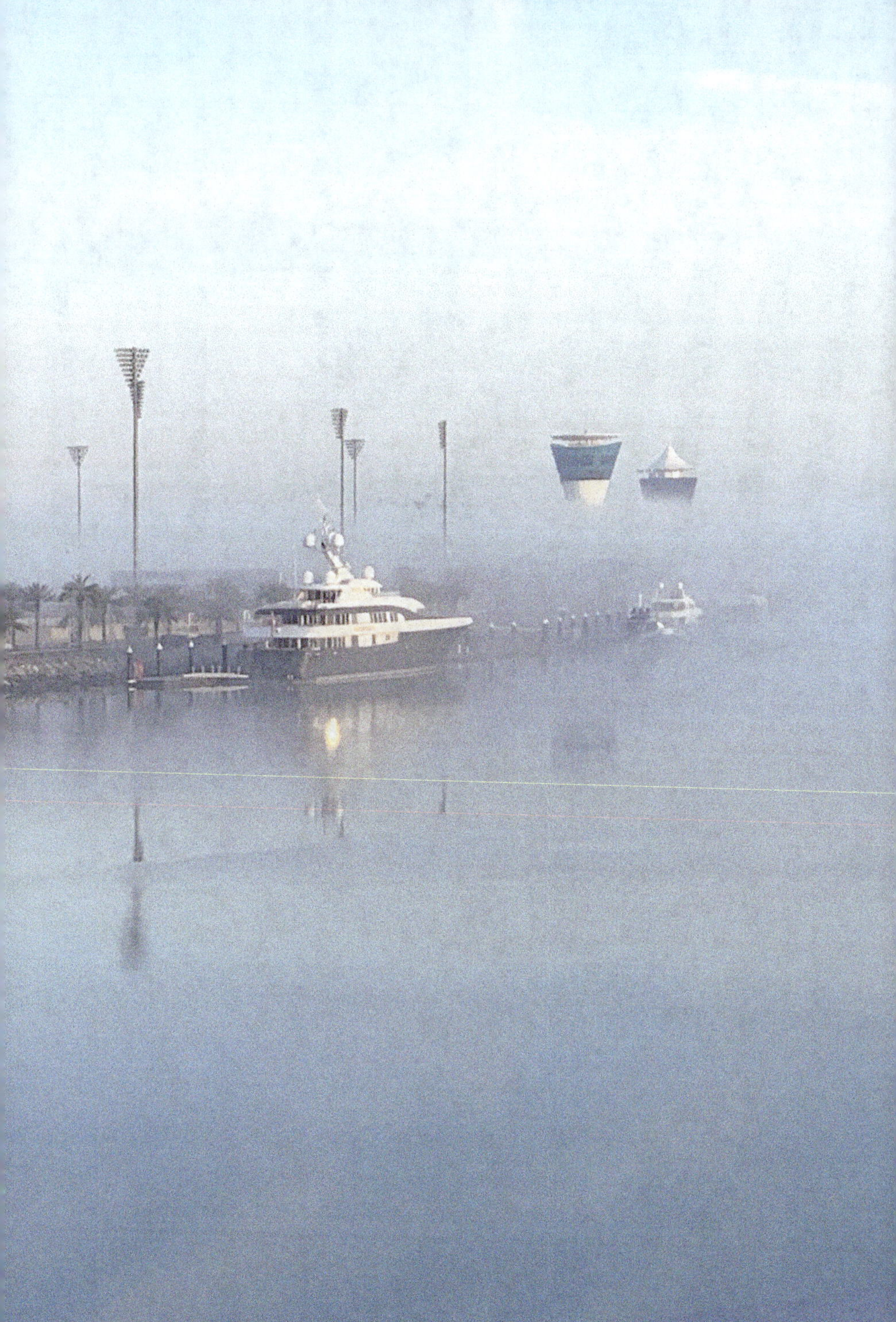

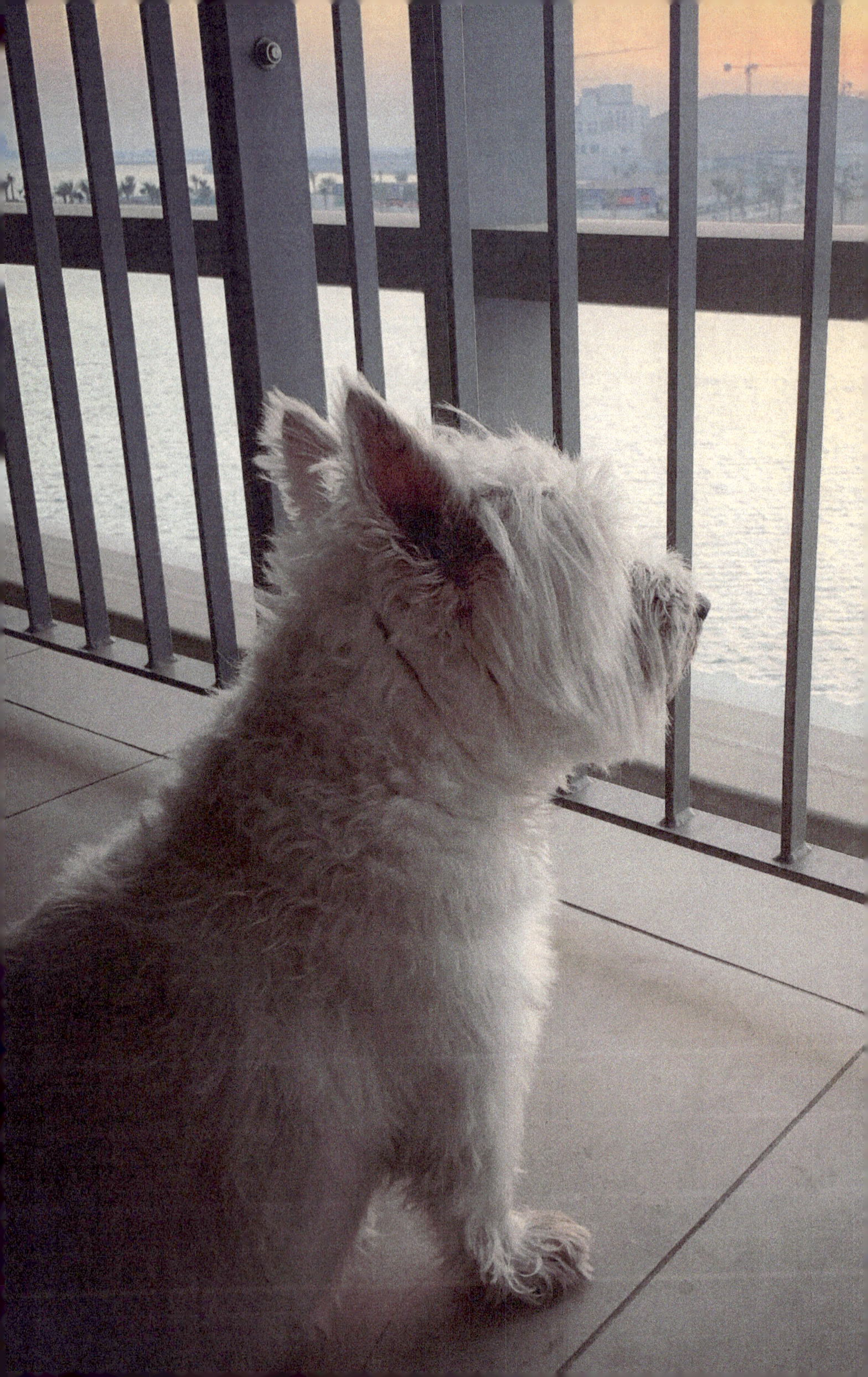

QUARANTINIS ON THE BALCONY

I moved to Dubai five years ago, after my husband passed away and I lost my job. It was an exciting chance to start something new and eventually, I landed in the capital city of Abu Dhabi in a beautiful apartment with an amazing balcony overlooking the water. Every day I have enjoyed that view and spend as much time on my balcony as I can.

I turned 60 at the end of 2019, and had a plan to finish my five years in August 2020, take my savings and move to another developing country where I could spend my time on the beach, practice my photography or write. Less than two months later the COVID-19 virus changed the world and everyone in it. My life, like everyone's, was turned upside down; by the first of March the UAE had closed it boarders. No one could leave or come into the country because soon after we were put under "shelter in place" orders. We couldn't leave the house for any reason except a medical emergency or essential needs at the grocery store or pharmacy.

A colleague was staying with me, finalizing her exit out of the UAE and she was suddenly stranded. As a joke, we decided to start the Daily Quarantini so each day I made a new drink and took pictures of it off my beautiful balcony. About three weeks into our quarantine, my colleague moved on and I thought I would stop the daily ritual since it was just me at home. There was a public outcry! NO! We look forward to seeing your daily quarantini, please don't stop. My dad was the one who encouraged me by saying, you have the recipes and the pictures now tell the stories and write a book.

I hope you enjoy the cocktails, photos and anecdotes about being quarantined in the UAE.

Cheers!

CLASSIC GIN AND TONIC

2 oz premium Gin

7 oz Fever Tree
   Indian Tonic

Grapefruit
   (or other citrus fruit)
   for garnish

Pour gin over ice in a tall glass, followed by the tonic water. Squeeze a grapefruit slice over the drink and drop into the glass.

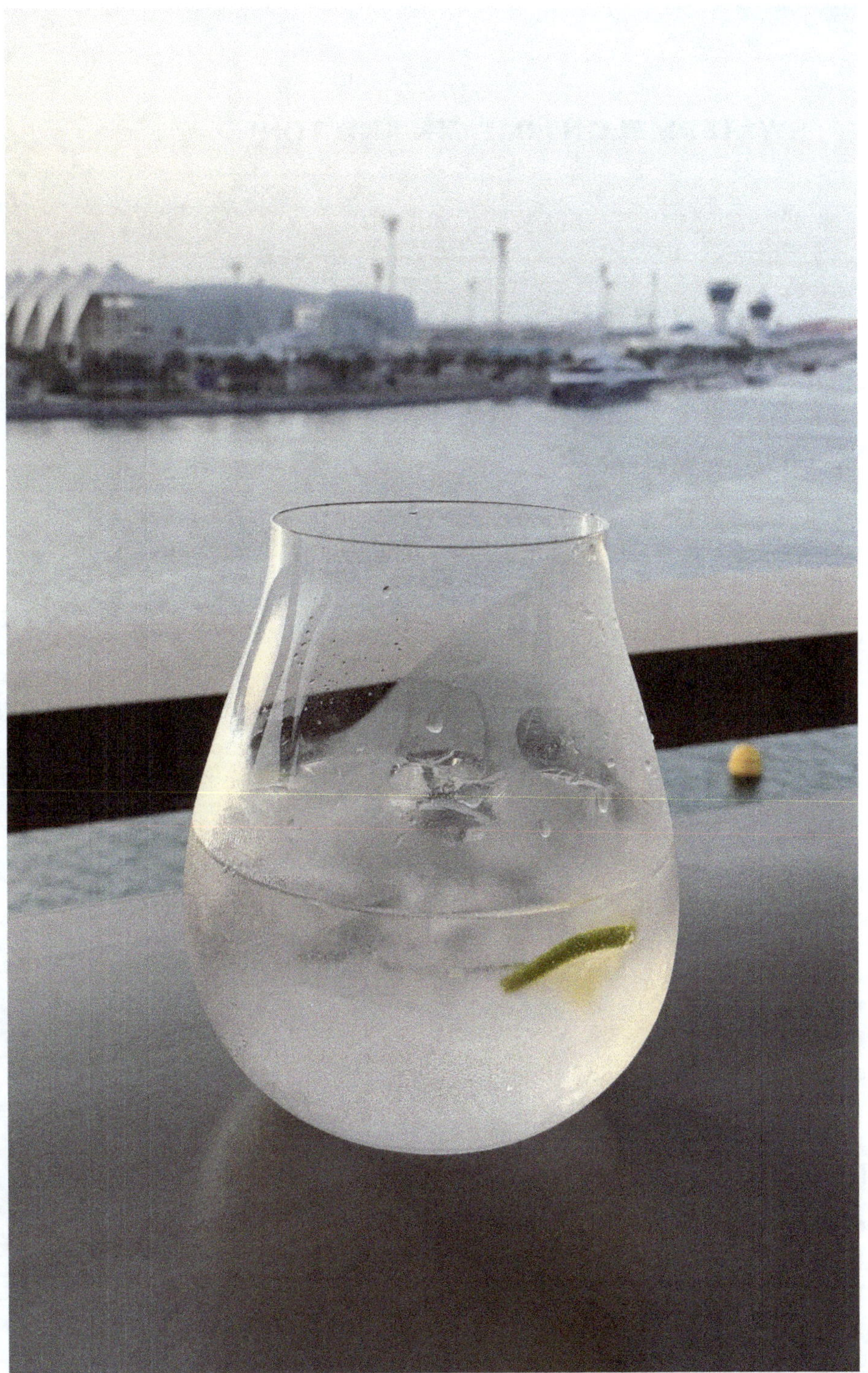

WATERMELON LIME GIN AND TONIC

2 oz Edinburgh Gin

Watermelon Lime Gin

*7 oz Fever Tree
Elderflower Tonic*

Watermelon cubes

Lime wheel

Pour gin over watermelon cubes in a tall glass, follow with tonic water. Squeeze lime over drink and drop into glass. Garnish with lime wheel and watermelon slice.

To make watermelon cubes, freeze fresh watermelon juice in ice cube trays. Use in place of ice cubes.

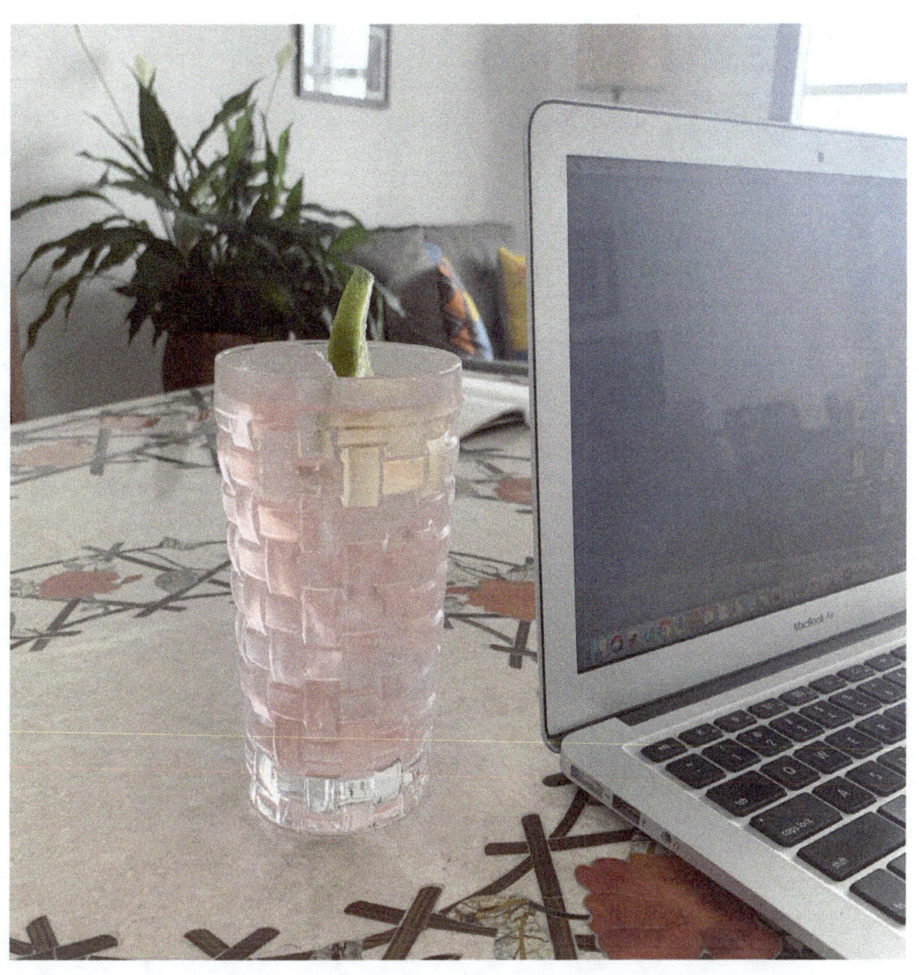

LOVE ON THE ROCKZ

2 oz gin

Fever Tree Indian Tonic Water

Lime wedge

Rosemary sprig for garnish if desired

2 tbsp blackberry syrup

2 thyme sprigs

Blackberry syrup

5 oz fresh blackberries

3 ½ oz granulated sugar

3 ½ oz water

Zest of 1 lemon

Fill a large rocks glass with ice. Pour in gin and cooled syrup, add a squeeze of lime and stir to mix. Garnish with a lime wedge or rosemary sprig.

To make the blackberry syrup, heat blackberries, sugar, and water in a sauce pan over medium-high heat until boiling. Reduce heat and let simmer for 20 minutes. Add lemon zest and thyme sprigs and leave to steep for 20 minutes. Strain through a fine mesh strainer and let cool.

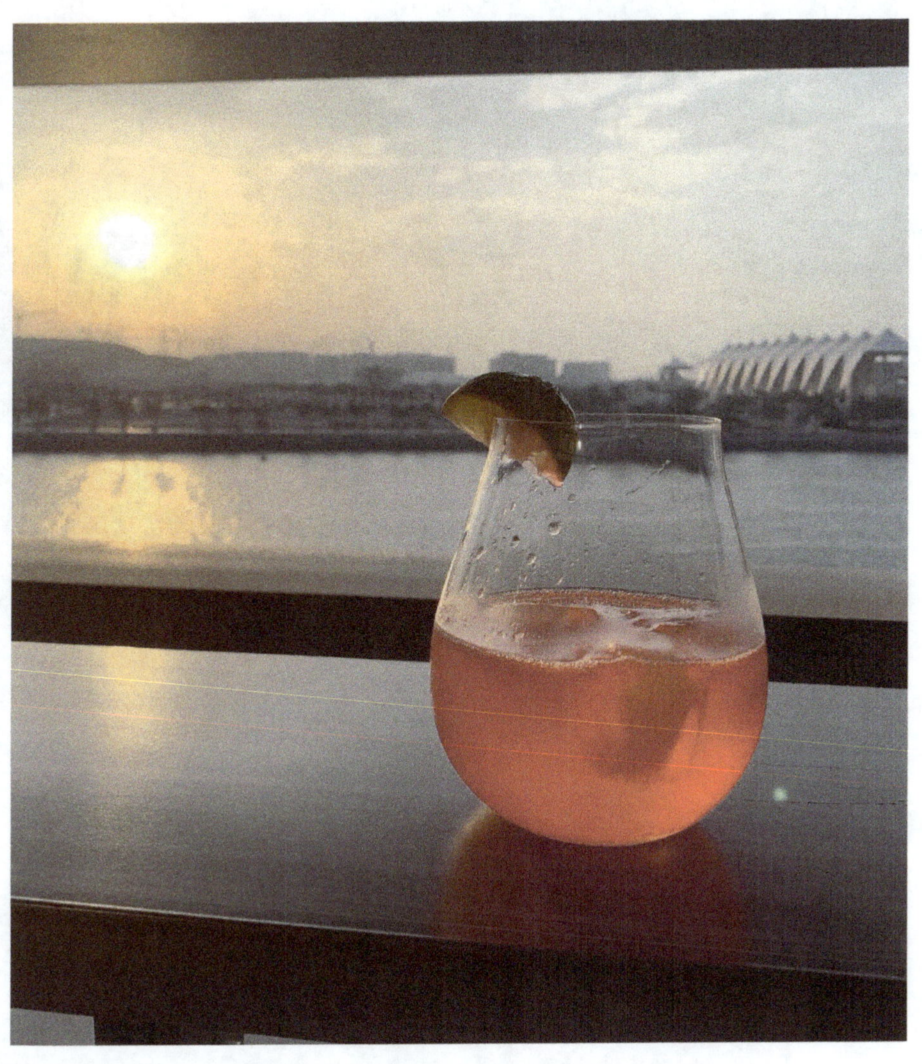

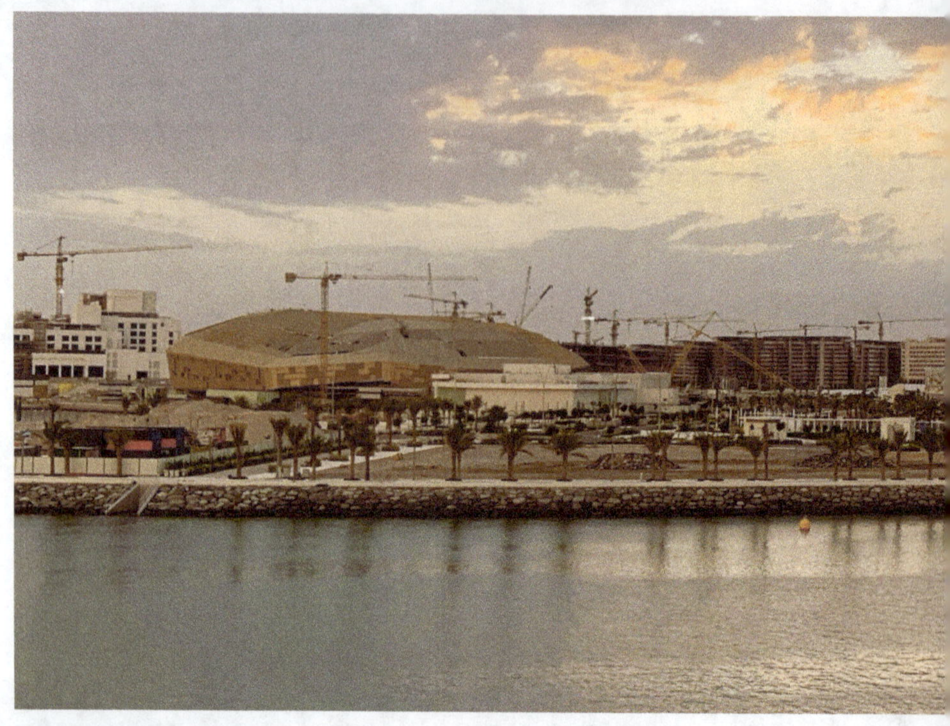

LOVE ON THE ROCKZ

The New Year started with friends and family and loads of festivities. It felt like 2020 was going to be MY year. I was on the bullet train to retirement after spending the last 5 years living and working in the Middle East. I didn't have a huge amount of money saved, but I got one son through Pharmacy school and the other son settled into a house in London; I had no debt and my financial planner assured me with a small push I could meet my retirement goals in three years. I felt stronger than I had since my husband, Brian, died. I was confident that finally, I had arrived.

By the end of February, the landscape started to change. I was just back from a Nile Cruise with my mom and she had developed an upper respiratory infection. My brother was arriving that day and we went to a walk-in clinic where we learned there was concern about a Coronavirus. Of course, I knew of reports about the virus outbreak in China over the past several weeks and I didn't really think much of it. The walk-in clinic treated my mom with some over the counter medications and sent us on our way to pick up my brother from the airport.

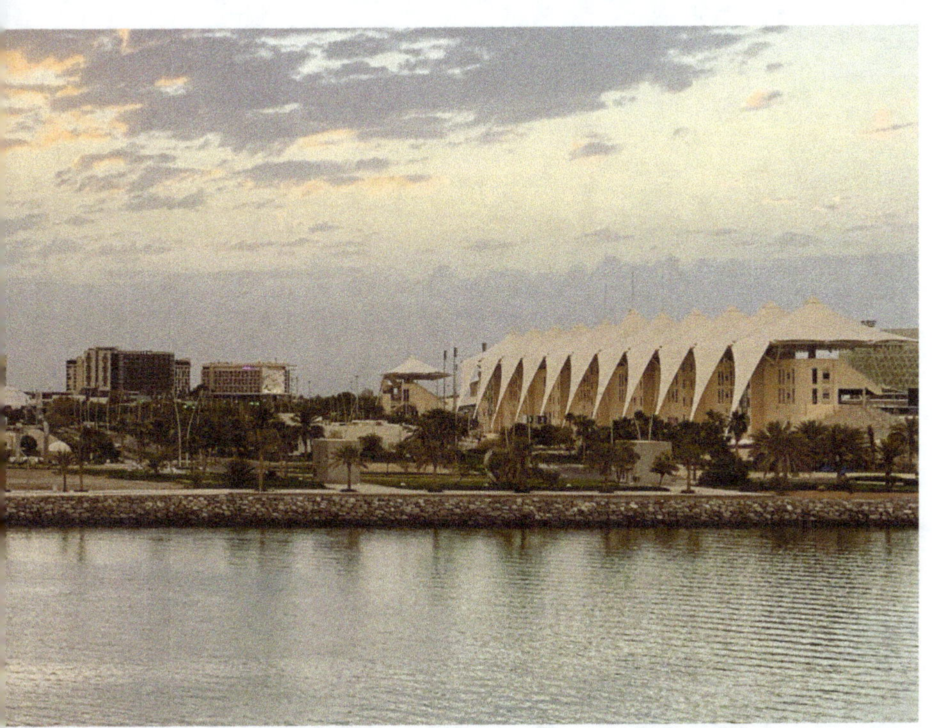

His visit started with three days in Dubai as planned, except by then my mom was coughing, had a fever and generally felt like a truck hit her. She stayed in the hotel room for three days and we did the touristy stuff on our own. On our way back to Abu Dhabi, I made arrangements for her to see my doctor at a local hospital where her medications were changed and COVID possibility was discussed. The doctor didn't feel that it was necessary to do the test as UAE was not really seeing cases yet. My mom improved and both she and my brother went back to the US by the end of February.

I was just getting settled back into my routine when out of nowhere the cloud of COVID fell over the UAE like a heavy fog. The weather had been very dusty and we seldom saw the usual crystal-clear blue sky. Now there was talk of people getting sick with the same virus that virtually closed China. At first it seemed impossible that could happen here. Nothing ever really crosses the borders of the UAE that does much harm so how could this be any different? My friends and I continued our dinners out, our lunch meetings, our happy hours thinking it would pass quickly and be no big deal. Were we ever wrong!

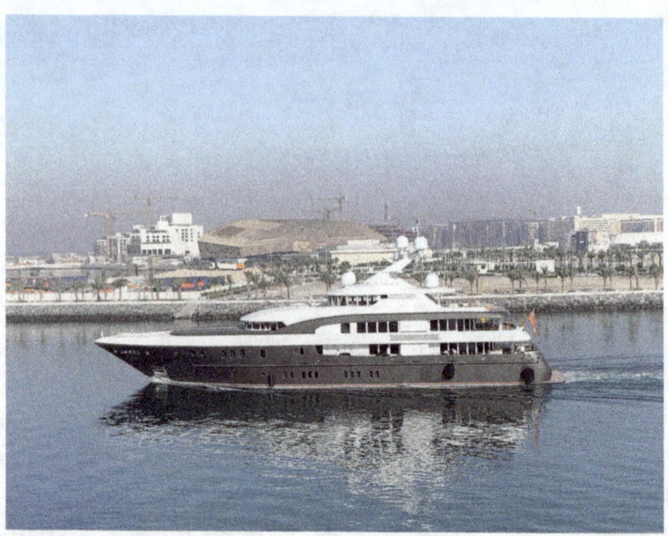

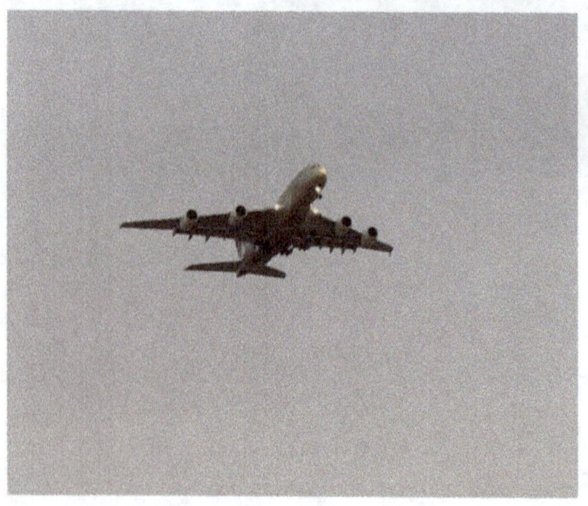

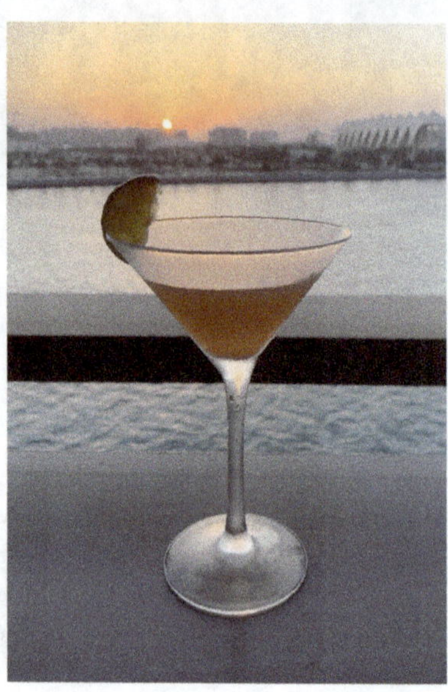

By mid-March strange things started to happen. First, they set up thermal cameras in the malls. They closed the nightclubs and the bars. The government started issuing orders about travel bans and curfews and before we knew it the whole world turned upside down. Malls, cinemas, and amusements parks closed first. Then parks, restaurants, beaches and some services. This was followed by a curfew where we were not allowed to move about for 10 hours over night and eventually every single thing was closed except grocery stores and medical care. The curfew was extended to 12 hours; then a full lockdown was put in place prohibiting you from leaving the

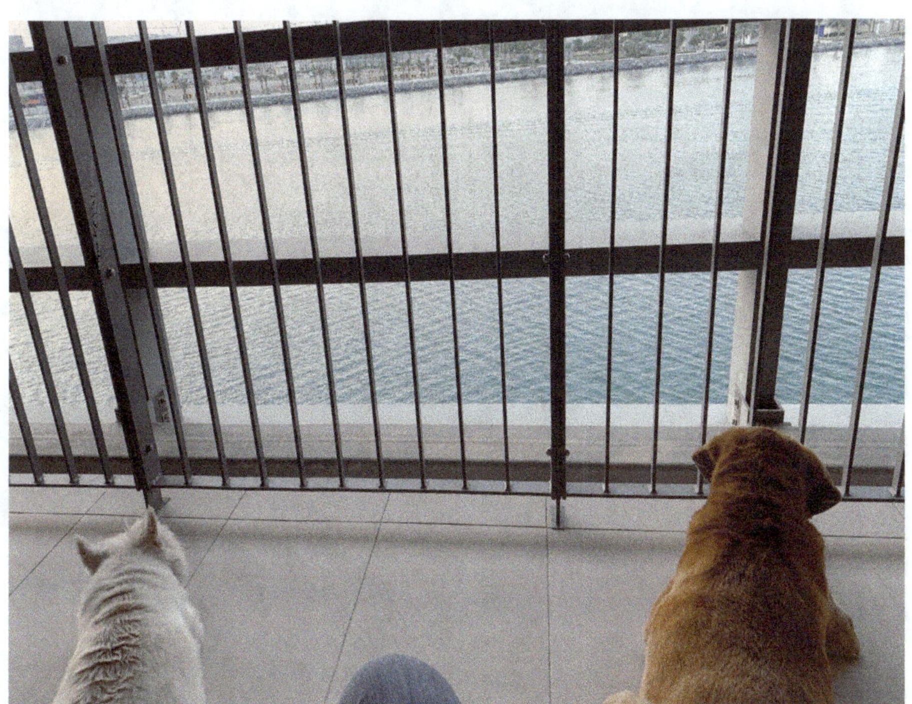

house for any reason that wasn't essential. You needed to register with the government to declare what was essential or risk a very hefty fine and possibly jail. That is when it started to sink in... this year was definitely not going to be my year.

Tara resigned at the end of February and Cheryl left to go to the US on annual leave at the same time. I was dreading the fact I would have to face the clinic job alone but it was only for a couple of weeks. Tara and I met at the mall near her apartment and my office for lunch a couple of times. Somehow our lunches started to include a cocktail or glass of wine even on work days. We talked about the seriousness of the new corona virus and what it might mean for the people that work for us and the people that rely on us

for care. I am an executive for an outpatient clinic that sees chronic disease patients exclusively. We discussed that really, our patients could be managed even if the clinic was entirely closed and perhaps that would be the right approach now. The CEO and the Medical Director had been recently let go and replaced by people with no experience in these roles. The new CEO had only been to the clinic a few times and with the start of this scare she wasn't coming to work at all. The new medical director was not even oriented to his role and having to make decisions affecting 700 staff and thousands of patients. His nerves were on edge from the very beginning of this. About two weeks into March, things had really ramped up in the UAE. More and more cases were being detected.

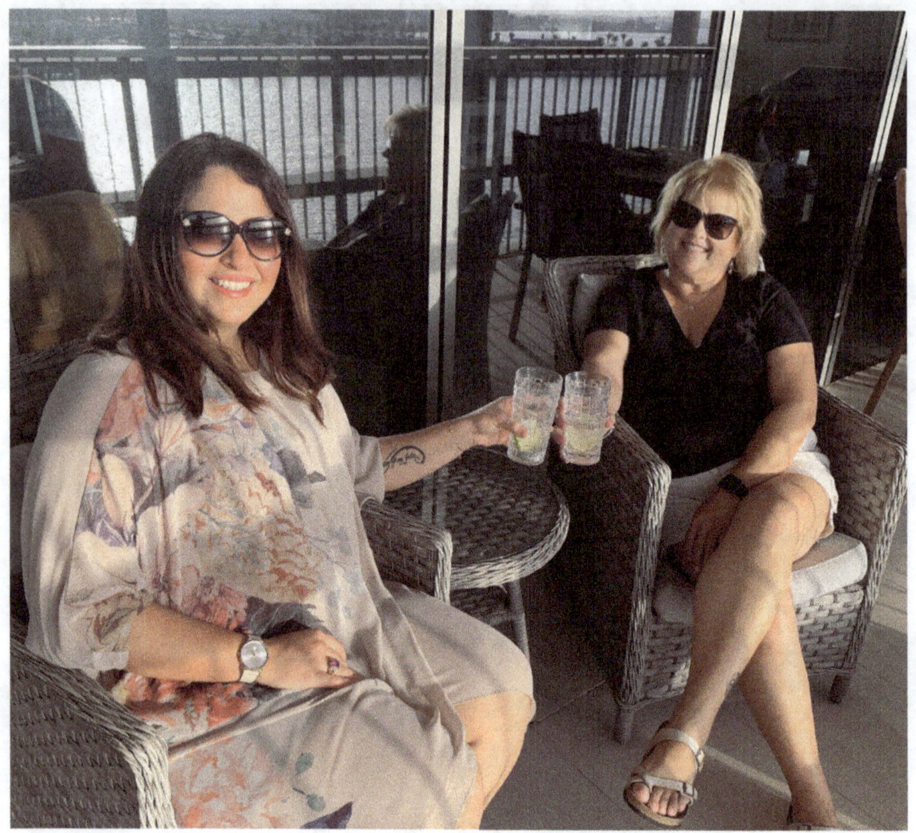

Fears of our clinic being infected created a panic with everyone. Human Resources was letting anyone who was pregnant, with kids, with immunocompromising conditions, etc. stay home. Of course, everyone else was trying to find a way they could stay home too. The level of fear and uncertainty was palpable everywhere by now. Most things around us were completely closed. Tara's lease was up and she came to stay with me for what we both thought would be only a few days. Cheryl was making her final preparations to return when the announcement came – all inbound and outbound passenger flights were cancelled.

The US was just starting to see cases of the virus on both the east and west coasts. There was a lot of confusion and misinformation about what was happening. Cheryl was due to leave the US just a few days before Tara was supposed to leave the UAE. Both of them were now in limbo. Tara was denied a visa to enter Vietnam where she intended to stay as a digital nomad for 6 months. Cheryl's residency visa in the UAE was put on hold. Now there were no flights to either place and even so, no visas to allow lawful entry. I had planned to join my son and daughter in law in Mumbai and then Goa for a close friend's wedding. As we

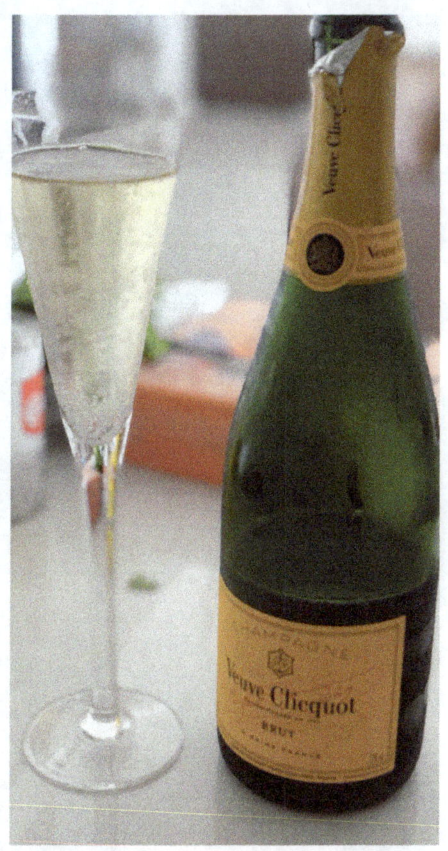

brunches, shopping and travel that made this all bearable once are barely a memory at this point. It sounds so ridiculous to say that because so much has happened to so many people all around me that is much worse than not being able to have my guilty pleasures. I am safe, I have plenty of food, there are no shortages and no long lines for anything. I have a job that pays me well enough to help others who have lost their jobs or have taken big reductions in pay. My friends and family are well and safe. But my life, like the life of most everyone around me, is on hold. Indefinitely. It is scary, and sometimes the responsibility for the safety and wellbeing of 100 nurses and 50 other ancillary staff is so heavy it hurts. People with families that need them are being asked to do things out of their comfort zone, out of their skill set, out of their ordinary life.

waited and wondered, it became evident, we could not get visas to enter India or flights to either city so plans were cancelled, the wedding postponed indefinitely and our lives essentially put on hold.

It's been almost 2 months since this started. A job that was already frustrating, disappointing, and generally unsatisfying has now become so bad I can barely sleep. My plans to resign and move back to the US are uncertain at best. The little pleasures of a manicure, pedicure, massage, beach days, pool time, happy hours, dinners,

There are so many unanswered questions
and so much information you can barely
take it all in. At the same time, you
have to fact check it and filter it and try
to understand what it means for your
patients and your caregivers. We have
little leadership at either the local or the
corporate level. It is draining and exhausting
and I spend many hours of my day cursing
the situation. Tara is stranded, luckily at
my house so she at least has a place to
stay and some creature comforts of home.
Cheryl is stranded in the US, luckily with
her adult daughters nearby but her beloved
cats are in the UAE. Everyone has a story
like this and many have someone close that
has been affected by COVID. This is not
the 2020 I envisioned. This is not MY year.

This week they announced some flights
would slowly resume to help people get
back to their home countries. China is slowly
returning to their lives of 10 weeks ago.
While the US has yet to see the peak, there
seems to be glimpses of hope all around.
Our cases in the UAE continue to climb
as well and there are no signs of returning
to our normal. In fact, I expect it to get
worse before it gets better. Until then, I look
for the humor in everything, take time to
appreciate the small things like my dogs,
or a video chat with my friends or family
and wait patiently. Brian always used to say,
"this too shall pass".

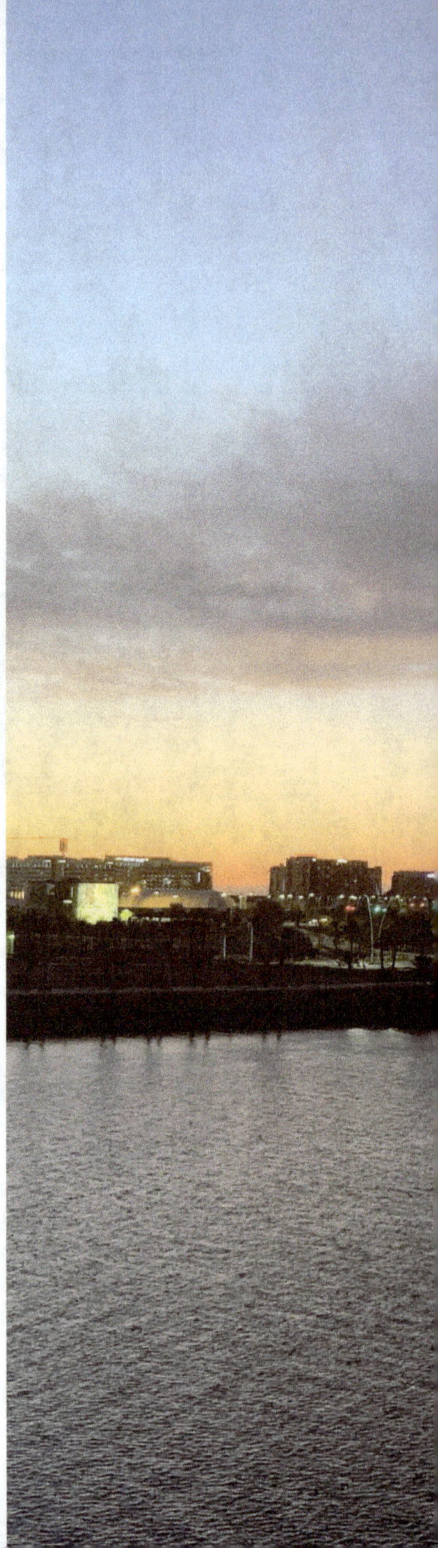

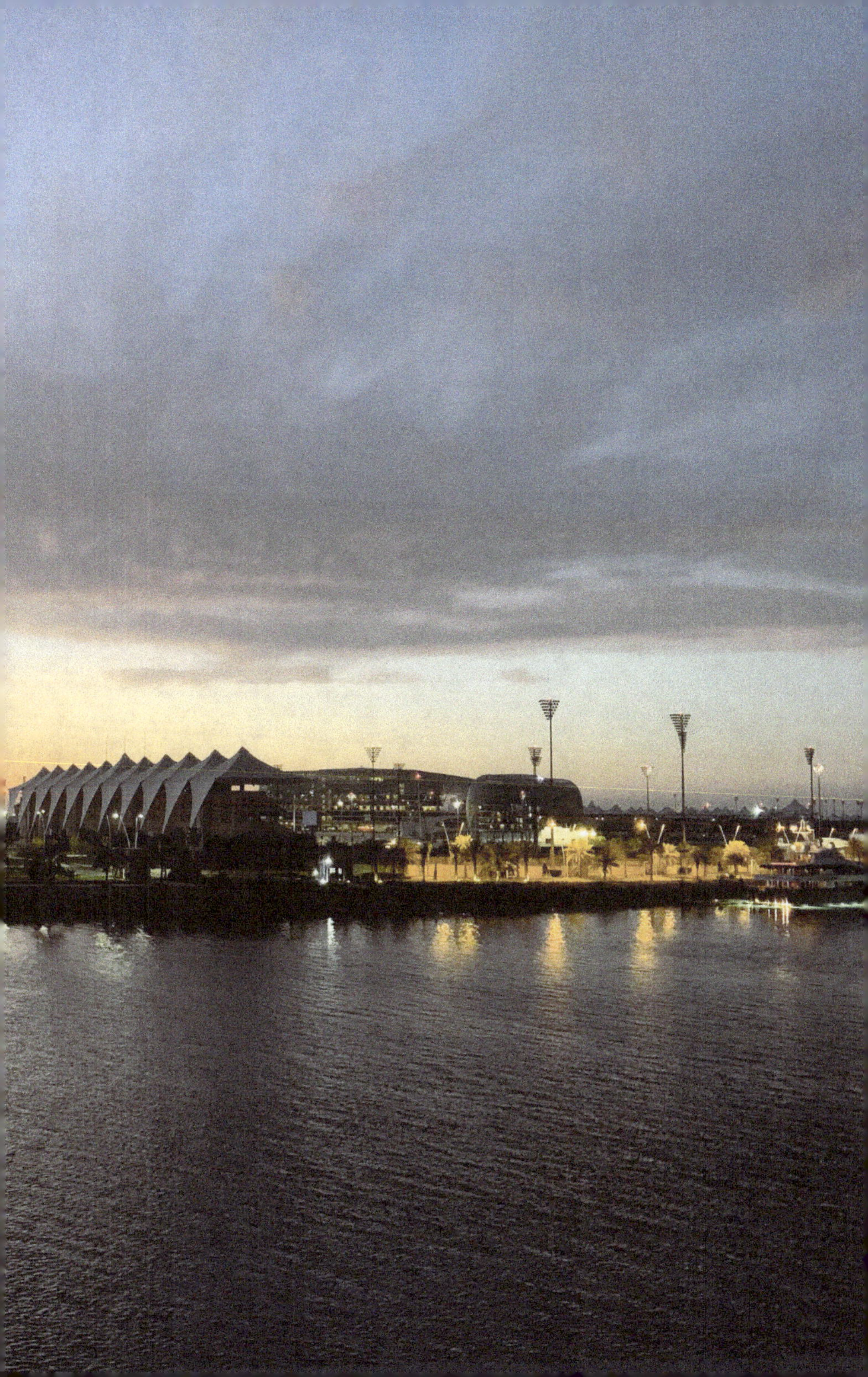

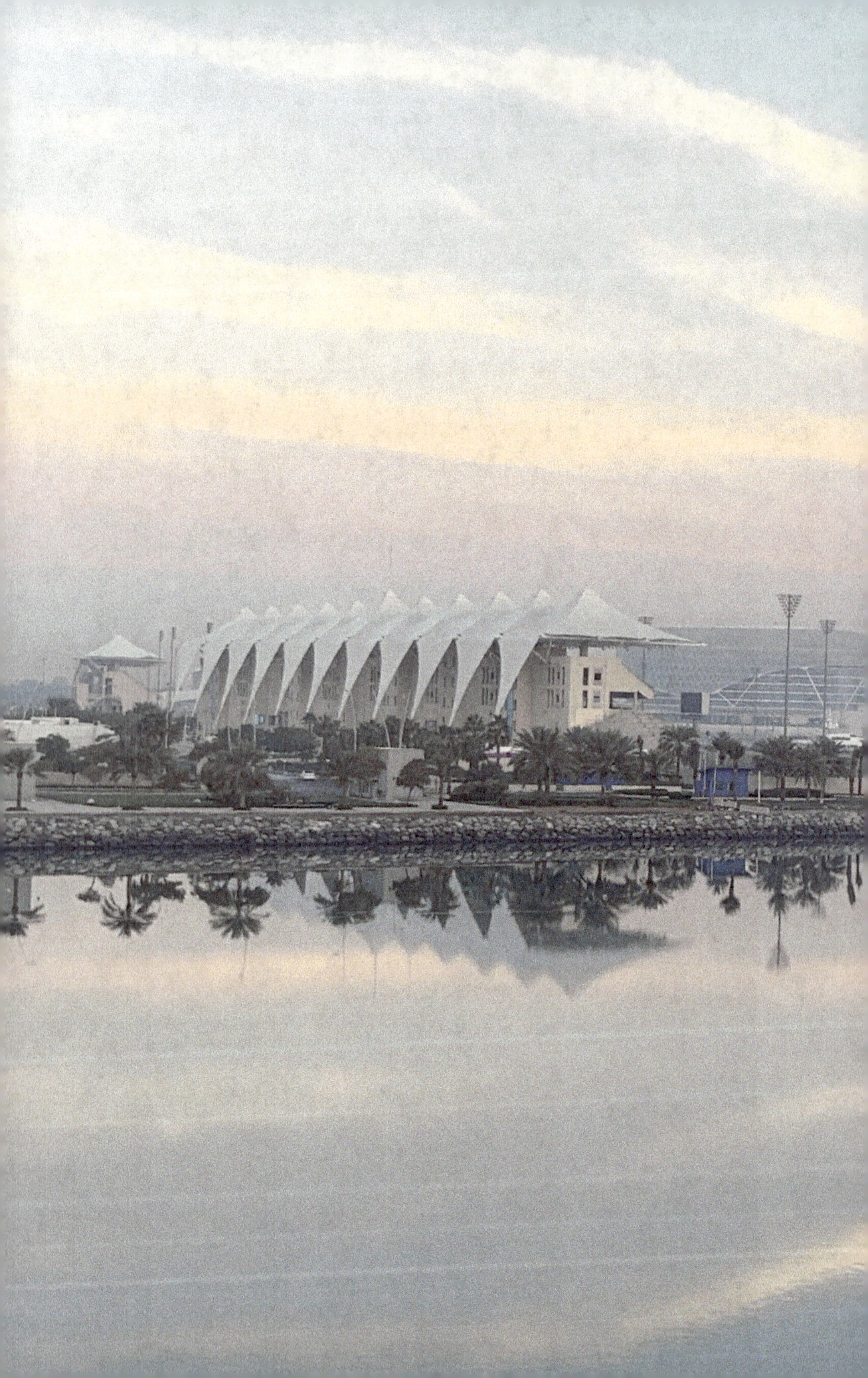

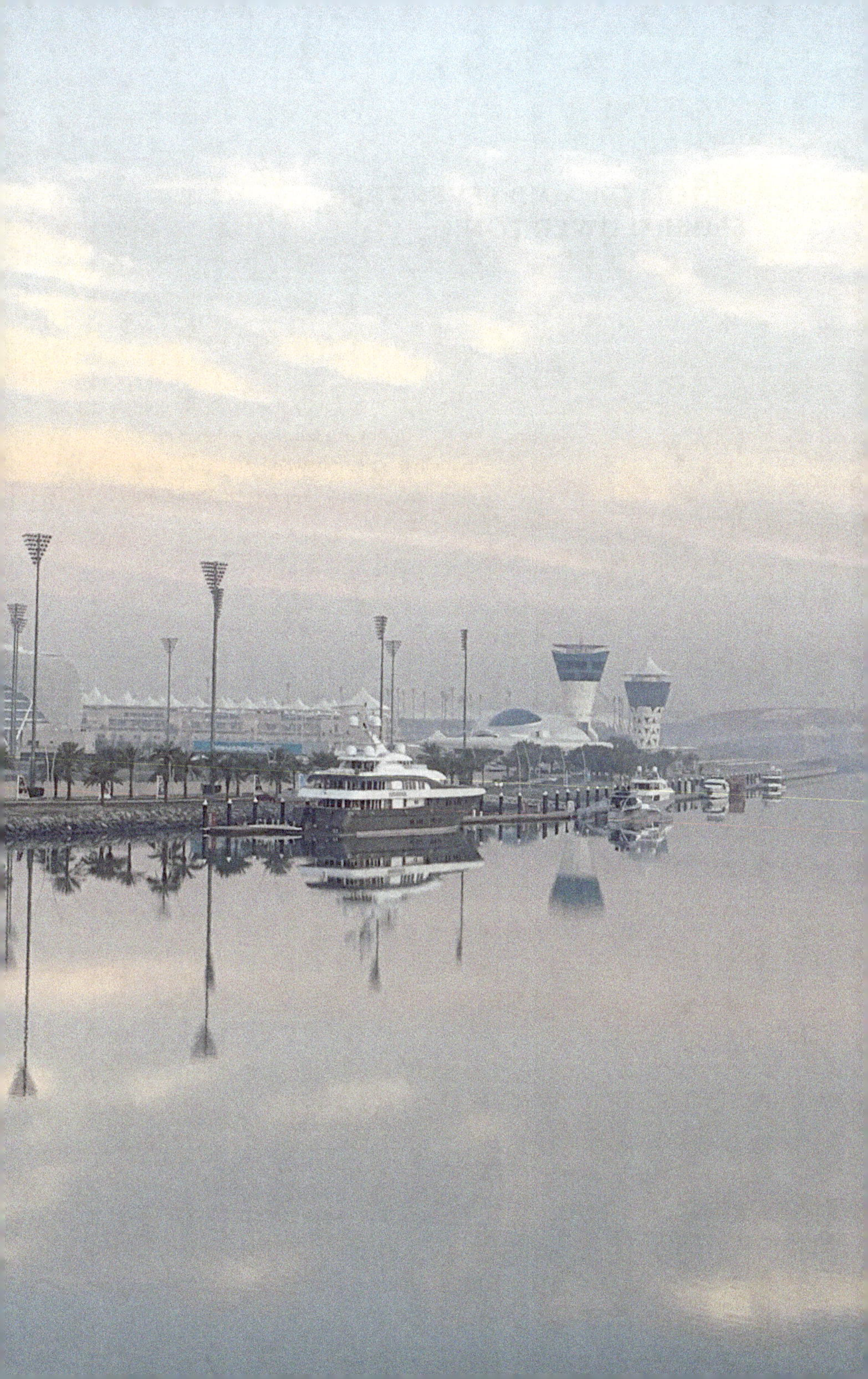

BLOOM GIN AND FEVER TREE ELDERFLOWER TONIC

2 oz Bloom Gin

5 oz Fever Tree
  Elderflower Tonic

Blueberries
  (or other fresh berries)

Pink peppercorns

Use a spoon to gently smash the blueberries in the bottom of a tall glass. Add ice and pour in the gin, followed by the tonic water. Sprinkle with pink peppercorns. Stir to mix.

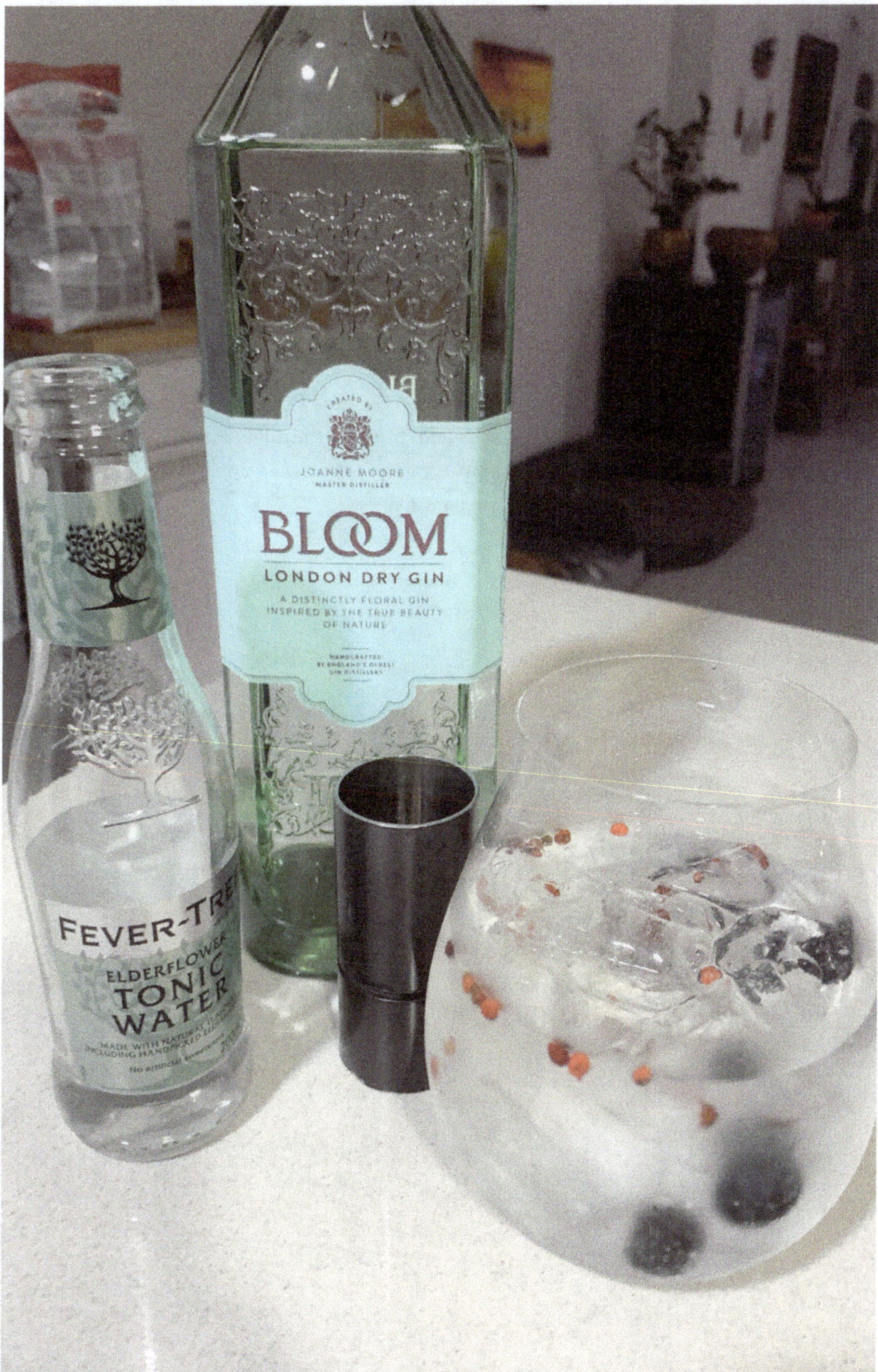

CREATED BY
JOANNE MOORE
MASTER DISTILLER
BLOOM
LONDON DRY GIN
A DISTINCTLY FLORAL GIN
INSPIRED BY THE TRUE BEAUTY
OF NATURE
HANDCRAFTED
BY ENGLAND'S OLDEST
GIN DISTILLERY
FEVER-TREE
ELDERFLOWER
TONIC
WATER
MADE WITH NATURAL FLAVOURS
INCLUDING HANDPICKED ELDERFLOWER
No artificial sweeteners

RHUBARB & GINGER GIN AND TONIC

2 oz Rhubarb
  & Ginger Gin

7 oz Fever Tree
  Elderflower Tonic

Citrus fruit wedge
  for garnish

Pour gin over ice in a tall glass, followed by tonic water. Squeeze a citrus wedge over the glass and drop into the drink. Garnish with a citrus wedge. Lemon or grapefruit work best, but lime is classic!

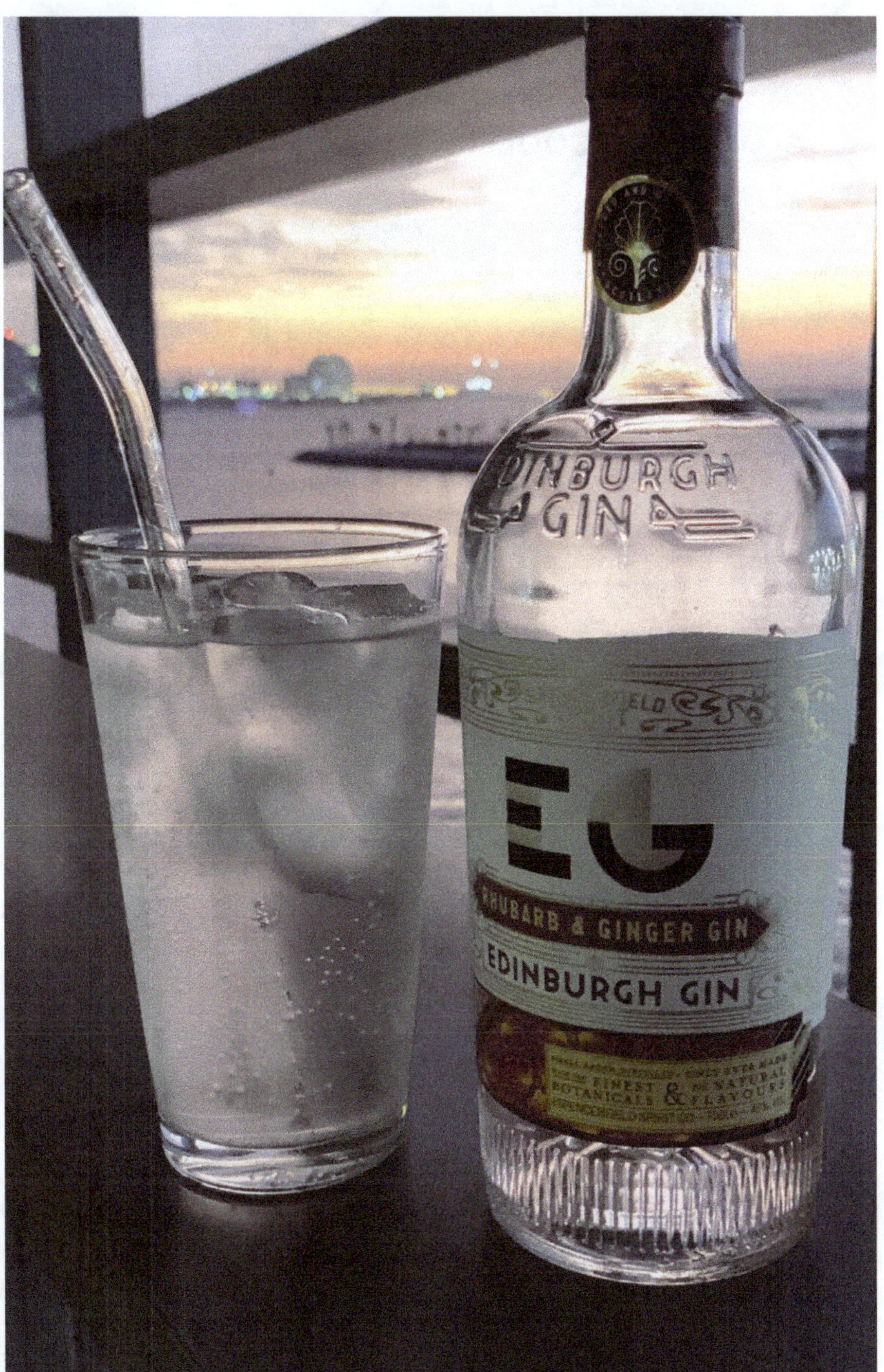
EDINBURGH GIN
EG
RHUBARB & GINGER GIN
EDINBURGH GIN
FINEST NATURAL
BOTANICALS & FLAVOURS

CLOUD SEED COOLER

2 oz premium gin

4-5 mint leaves

*Squeeze of fresh
  lemon juice*

*Squeeze of fresh
  lime juice*

1 ½ tsp limoncello

*4 oz Fever Tree
  Indian Tonic water*

Muddle the mint leaves with the limoncello in a tall glass. Add ice and pour in the gin, stir well. Add a squeeze of lemon juice and a squeeze of lime juice. Add the tonic water and top up the glass with ice. Garnish with a sprig of fresh mint.

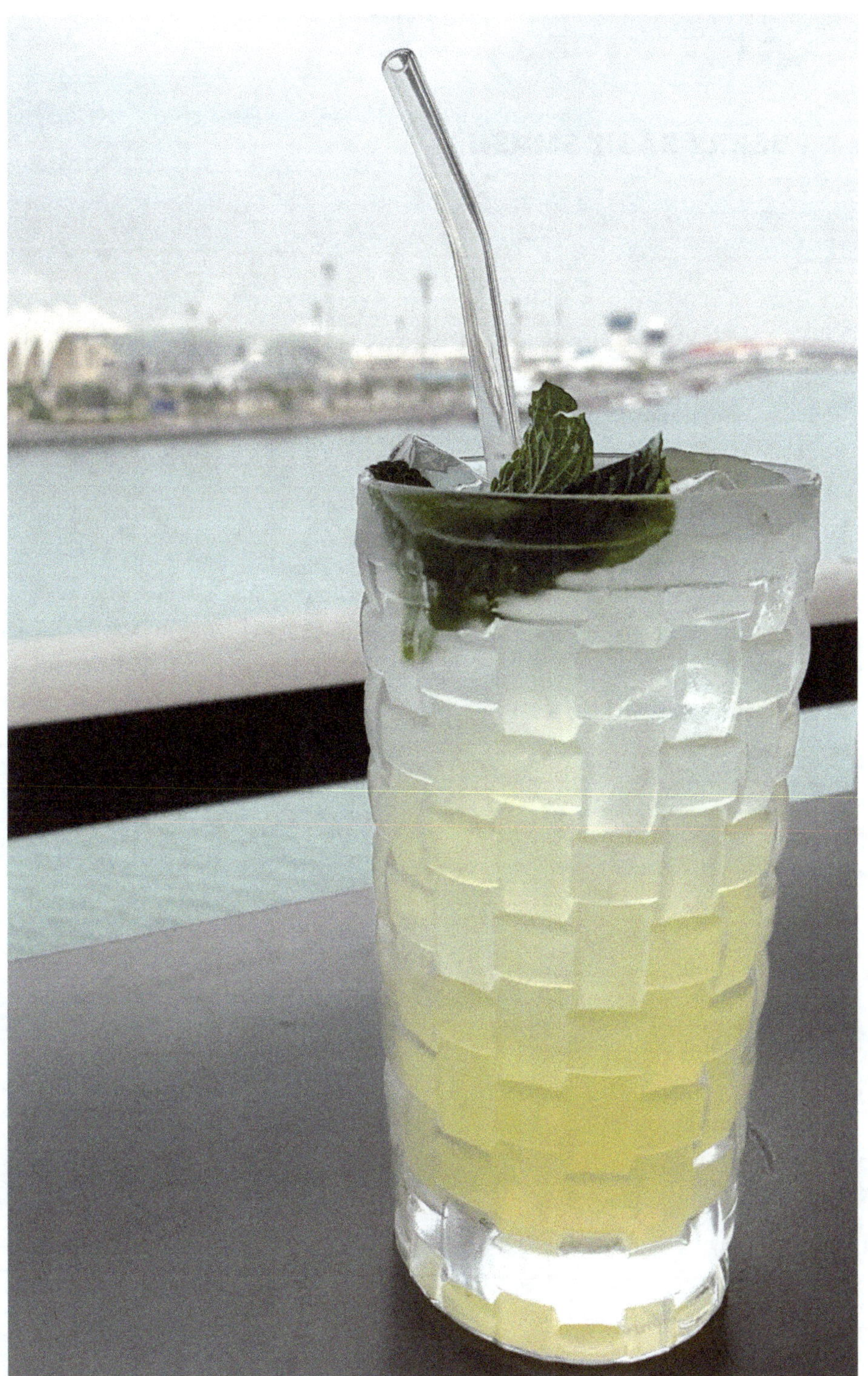

BERRY BASIL SMASH

2 oz gin

1 oz sparkling water

1 tbsp fresh lime juice

1 ½ tbsp raspberry basil simple syrup

Raspberries and basil leaves for garnish

Raspberry basil simple syrup

¼ cup granulated sugar

¼ cup water

6-10 whole fresh raspberries

3-4 leaves fresh basil

Pour gin, lime juice and simple syrup into a glass filled with ice. Add lime juice and stir gently to mix. Garnish with fresh raspberries and basil leave.

To make raspberry basil simple syrup, put raspberries, basil, sugar and water in a saucepan. Heat over medium heat until sugar is completely dissolved and berries are soft and juice is released. Pour into mesh strainer and press through to release raspberry juice and sugar water but strain seeds and basil leaves.

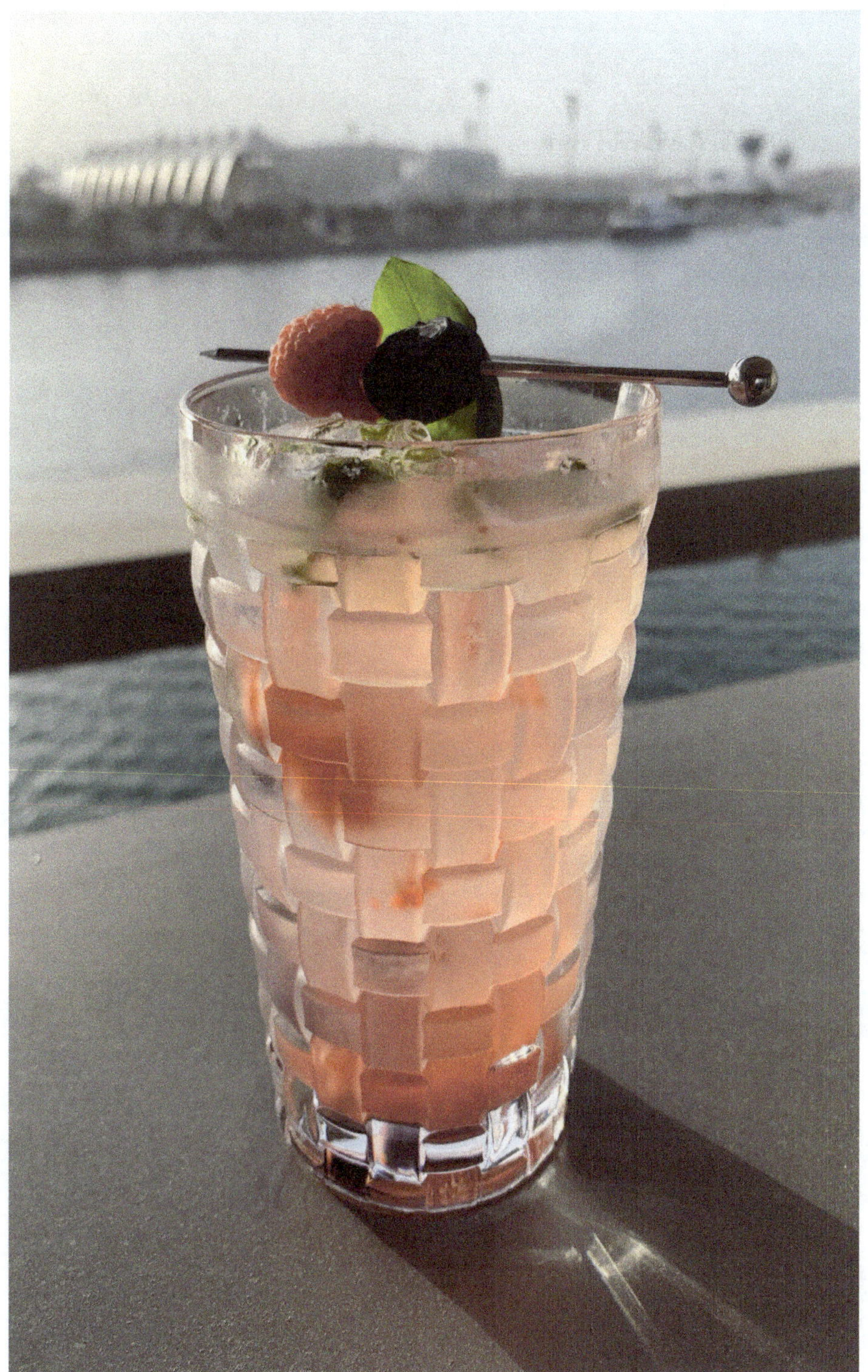

DIRTY MARTINI

2-3 hand stuffed blue cheese olives

2 oz premium vodka (gin can be substituted if you prefer)

¾ oz dry vermouth (optional and if left out add additional vodka or gin)

Splash of olive brine to taste

Pour vodka, vermouth and olive brine into cocktail shaker half full of ice and shake for 30 seconds until well chilled. Strain immediately into a chilled martini glass. Spear 2-3 olives on a decorative pick and place in drink as garnish.

To hand stuff olives, use large, pitted green olives and good quality blue cheese. Drain olives and pat dry with a paper towel. Use a small spoon or spatula to stuff the blue cheese into the open pit of the olive. Refrigerate before use.

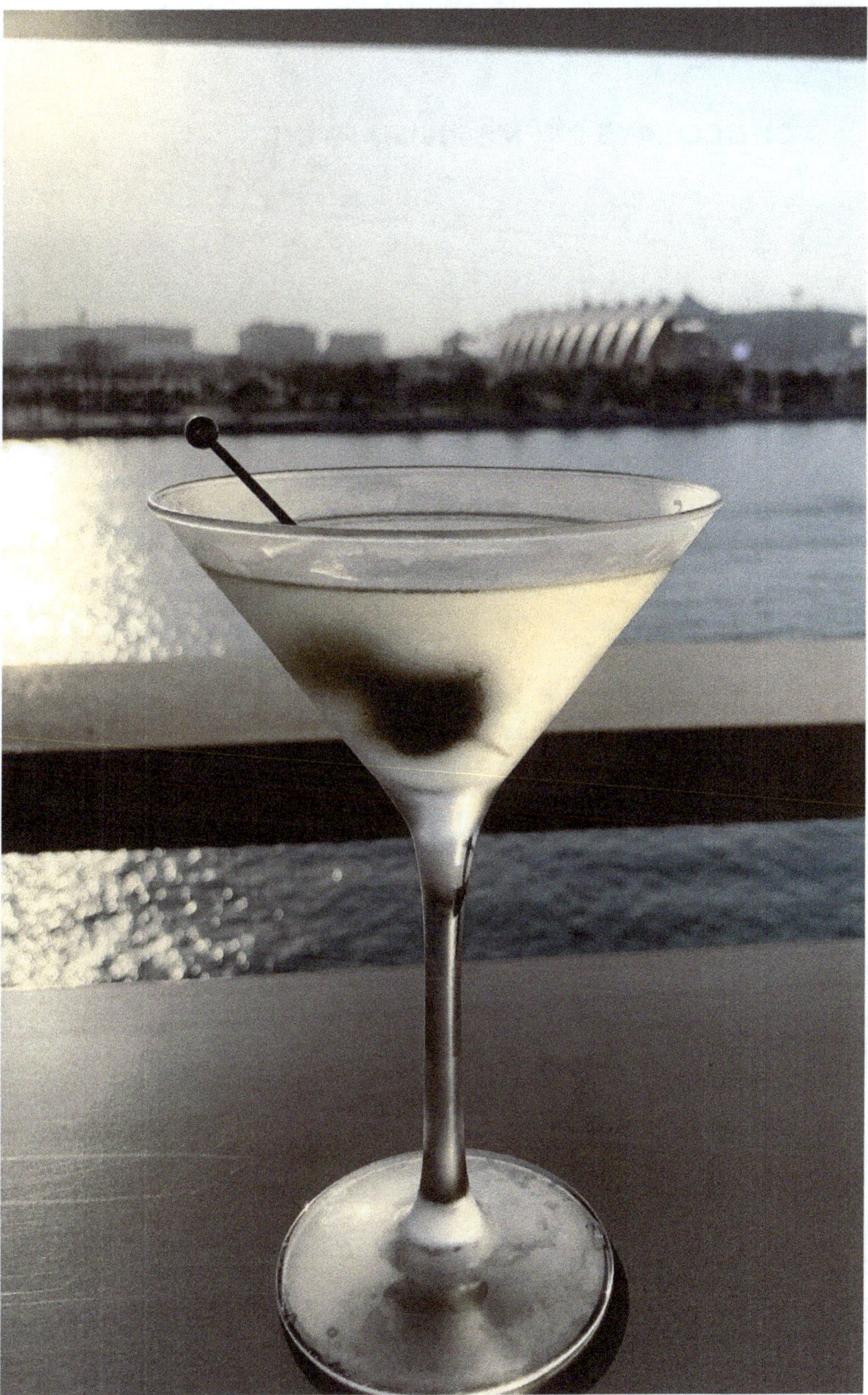

CHOCOLATE CRÈME PIE MARTINI

1 oz RumChata

1 oz good vanilla vodka

1 oz premium chocolate
  liqueur

1 tbsp chocolate syrup

Whipped cream

Maraschino cherries

Place ice, RumChata, vanilla vodka, chocolate liqueur and chocolate syrup in a cocktail shaker. Shake vigorously until well combined and chilled. Drizzle chocolate syrup into a chilled martini glass and pour the drink in immediately. Garnish with whipped cream and top with a cherry.

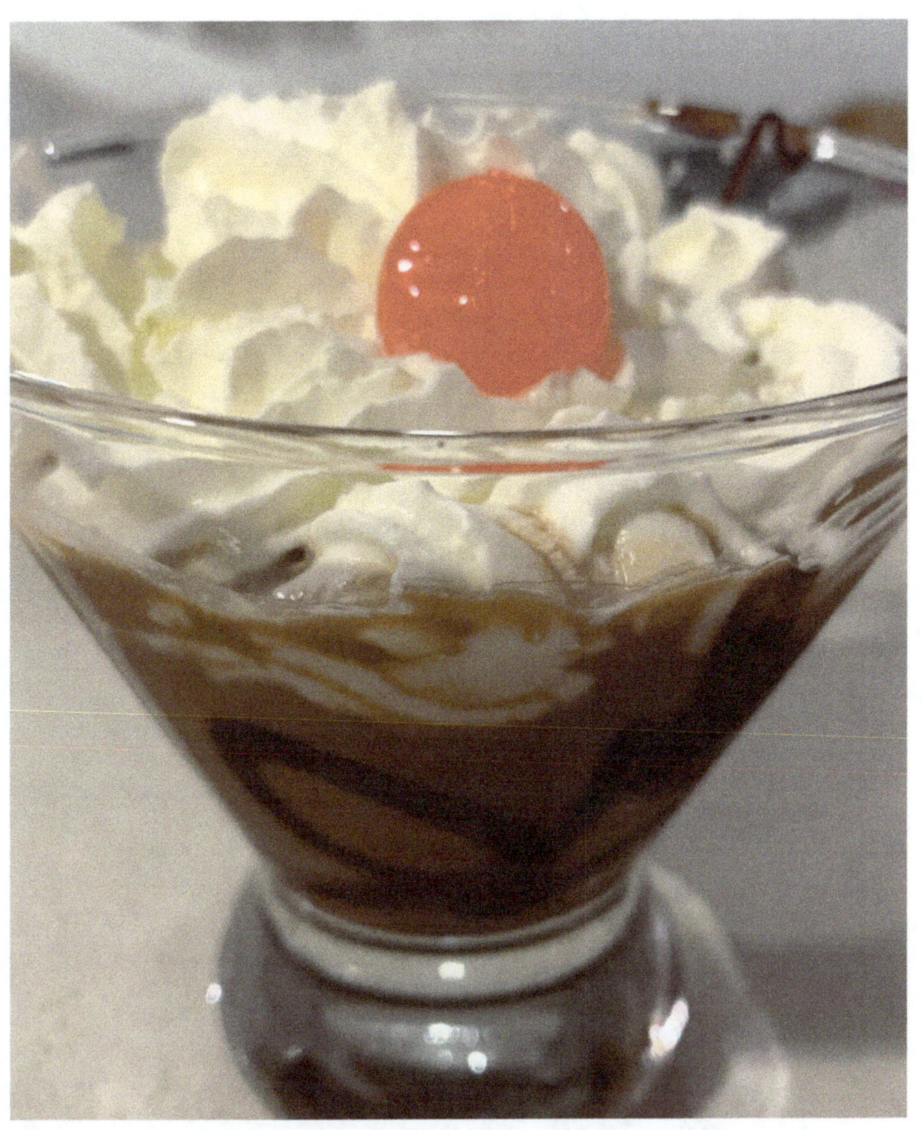

SCREWDRIVER

2 oz premium vodka

5 oz fresh orange juice

Splash of fresh mandarin
or fresh pineapple juice

Pour vodka over ice, followed by orange juice. Top with splash of fresh mandarin juice or fresh pineapple juice. Stir until well mixed.

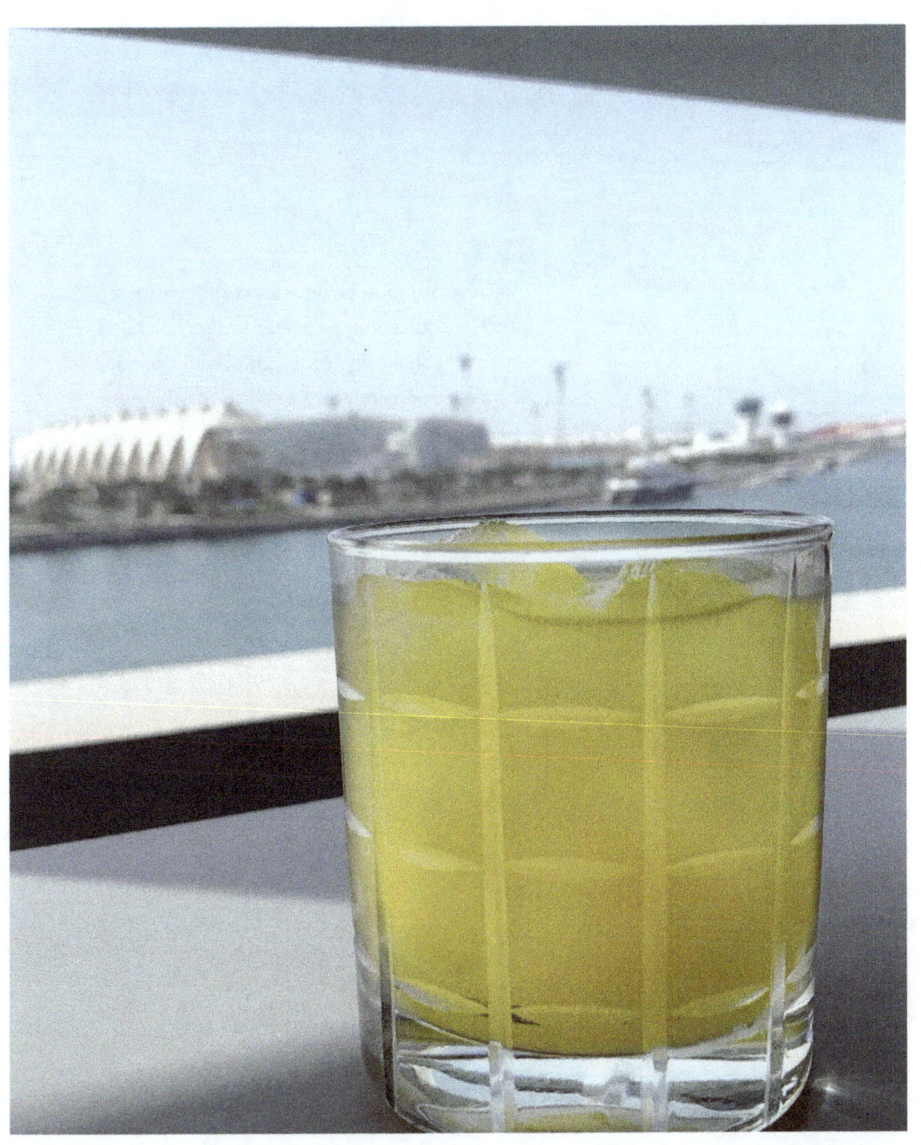

I NEED A KPI (COSMO) MARTINI

2 oz premium vodka

1 oz orange liqueur

*1 oz cranberry juice
cocktail*

½ oz fresh lime juice

Pour vodka, orange liqueur, cranberry juice and lime juice into a cocktail shaker half filled with ice. Shake vigorously until well chilled. Strain immediately into a chilled martini glass. Garnish with lime wedge.

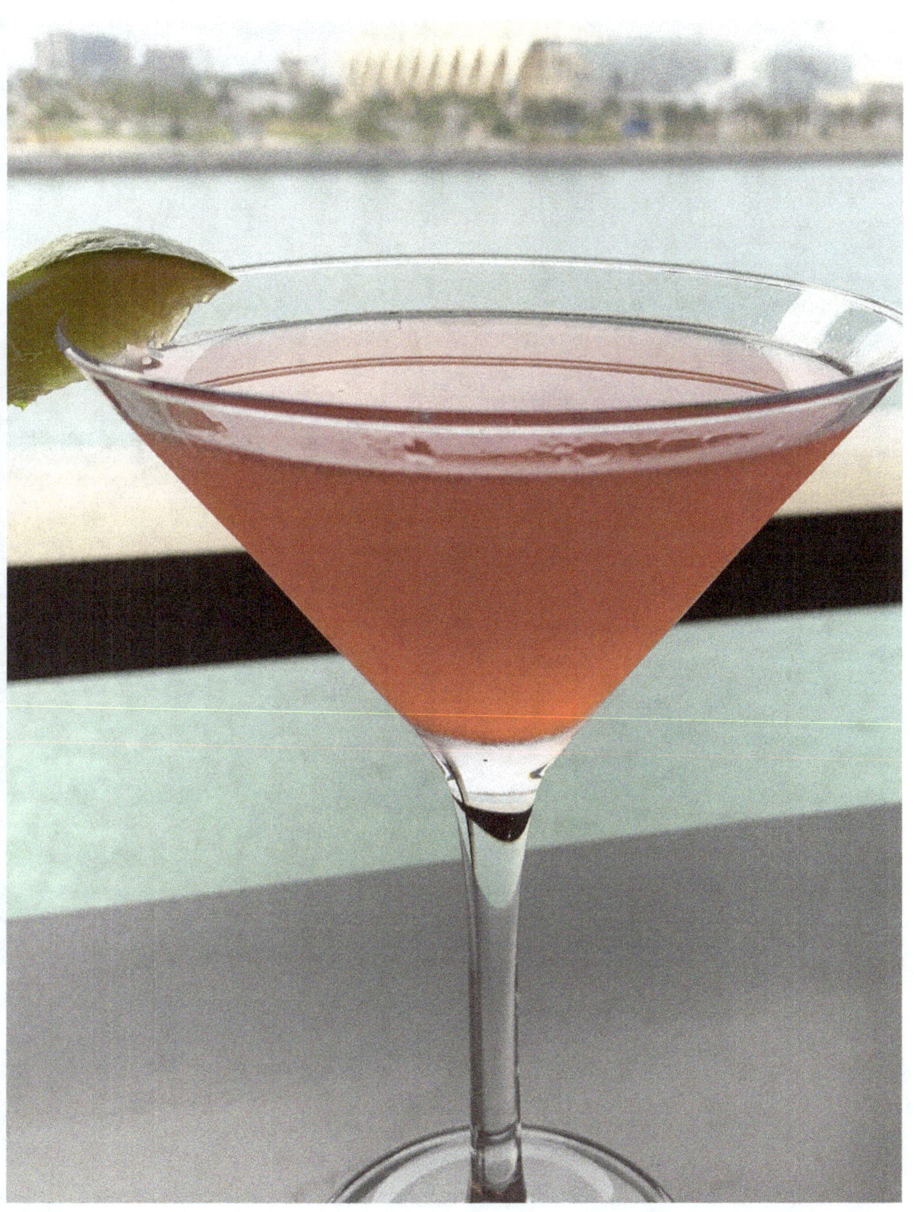

KPIs, COSMOS AND SUNSETS

As the Director of Quality for a large medical group in Abu Dhabi, I work with Key Performance Indicators (KPIs) on a regular basis. The COVID pandemic totally disrupted our day to day business and I had been working from my home office for about a month when my phone rang. Our newly appointed CEO was on the other end with a note of panic in her voice. She exchanged pleasantries and then blurted out "I need a KPI!". This struck me as absolutely hilarious and I had to control myself to keep from laughing out loud. My mind immediately started thinking, "why of course, let me reach into my drawer and pull one of those out".

After nearly five years working and living in the UAE, sometimes the simplest request or the most common course of conversation takes a turn that just makes you have to laugh out loud. That is the beauty of living as an expat, life doesn't always unfold the way you think it will or the way you are used to. Having this experience was so useful in dealing with the COVID pandemic.

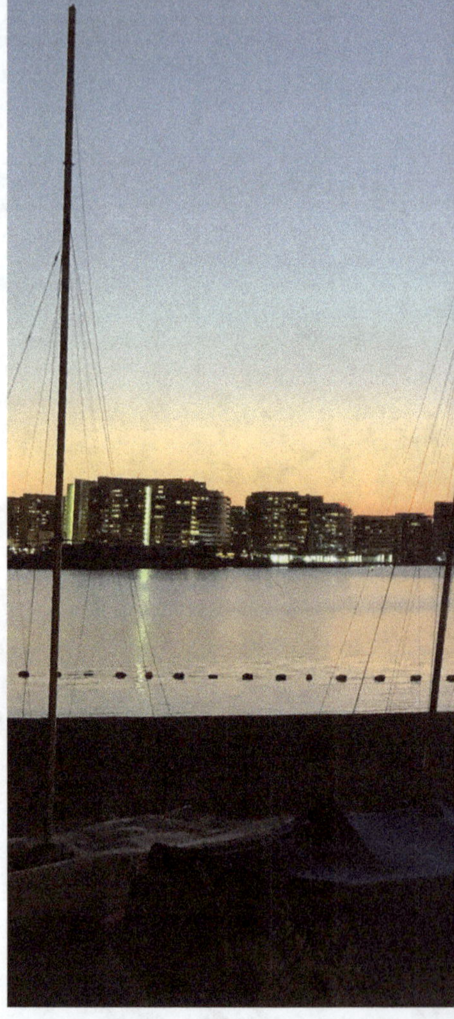

At first, my friends in healthcare and I thought this would last a couple of weeks and then everything would settle back down into our normal routine. Being able to work from home for a couple of weeks seemed like a dream to me. A couple of weeks has stretched into more than three months now and working from home, staying at home, being home all day, every day is not so dreamy anymore.

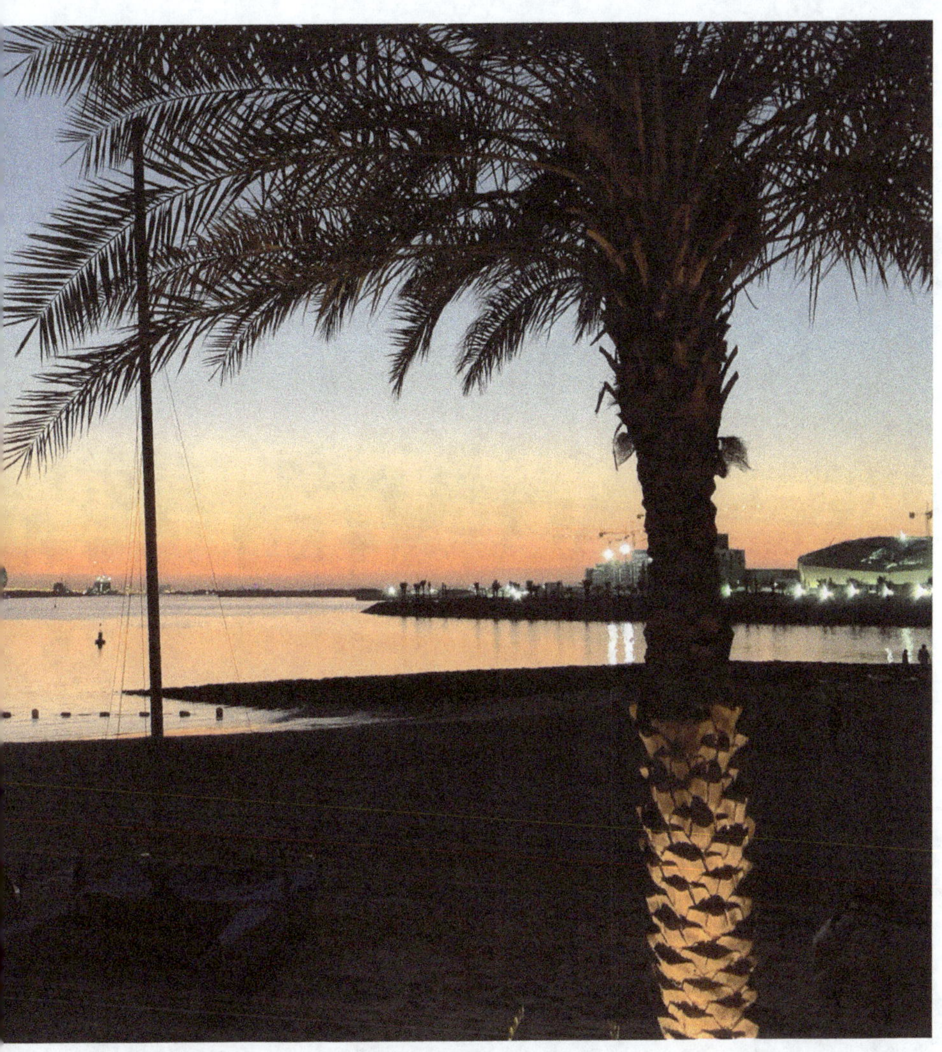

Once the initial panic and confusion wore off, the reality of how to manage things such as leaving the house only for groceries or an emergency became a way of life. Trips that had been planned and paid for had to be cancelled. Plans that were made months ago could not be executed. A trip to the grocery store required planning, to remember your mask and make sure you got there before a crowd gathered. Stand on the markings to keep you two meters apart, remember not to touch your face, use the hand sanitizer before and after you enter or leave the store. It was becoming a whole new way of life. Who had a KPI for that?

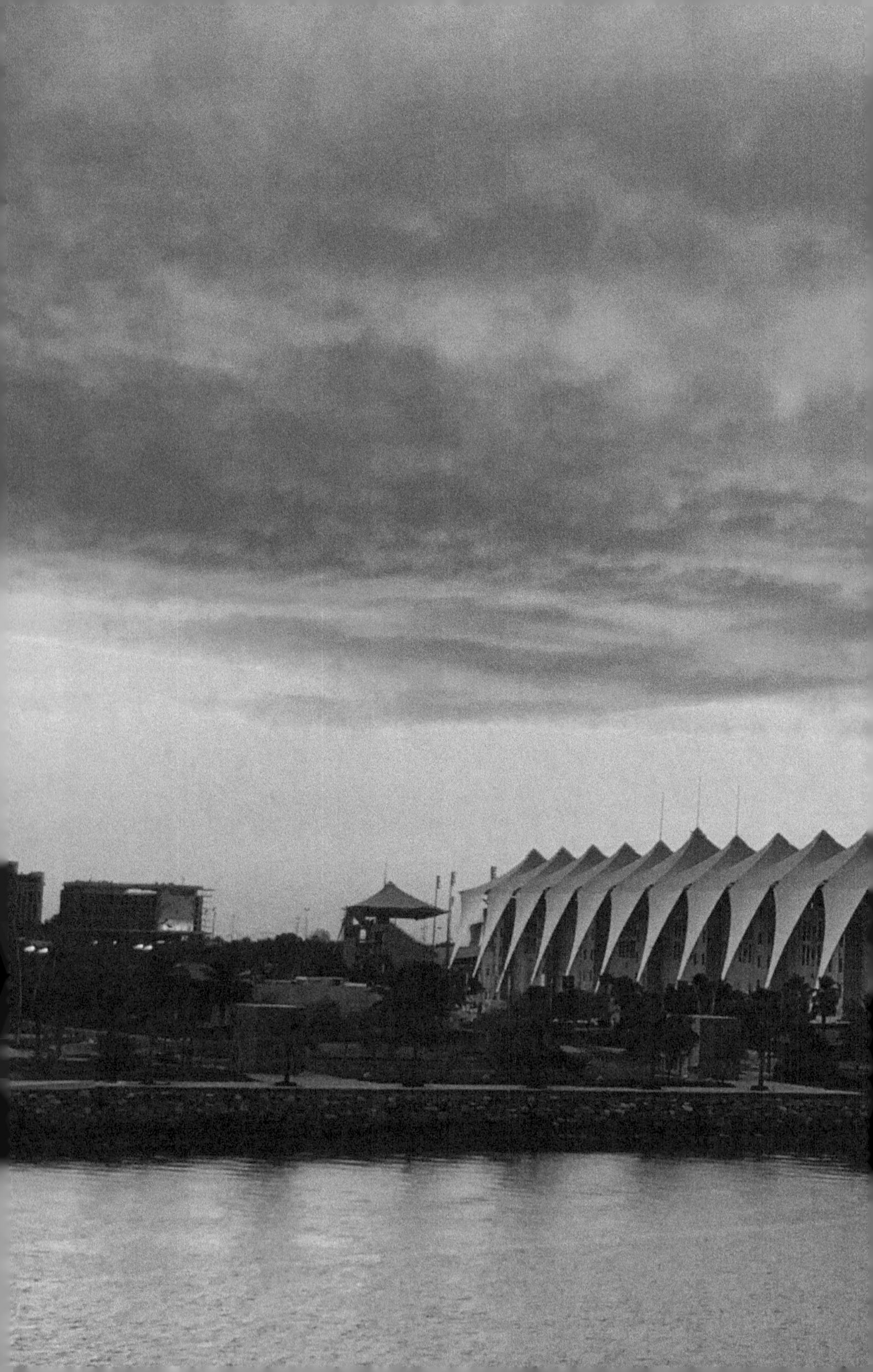

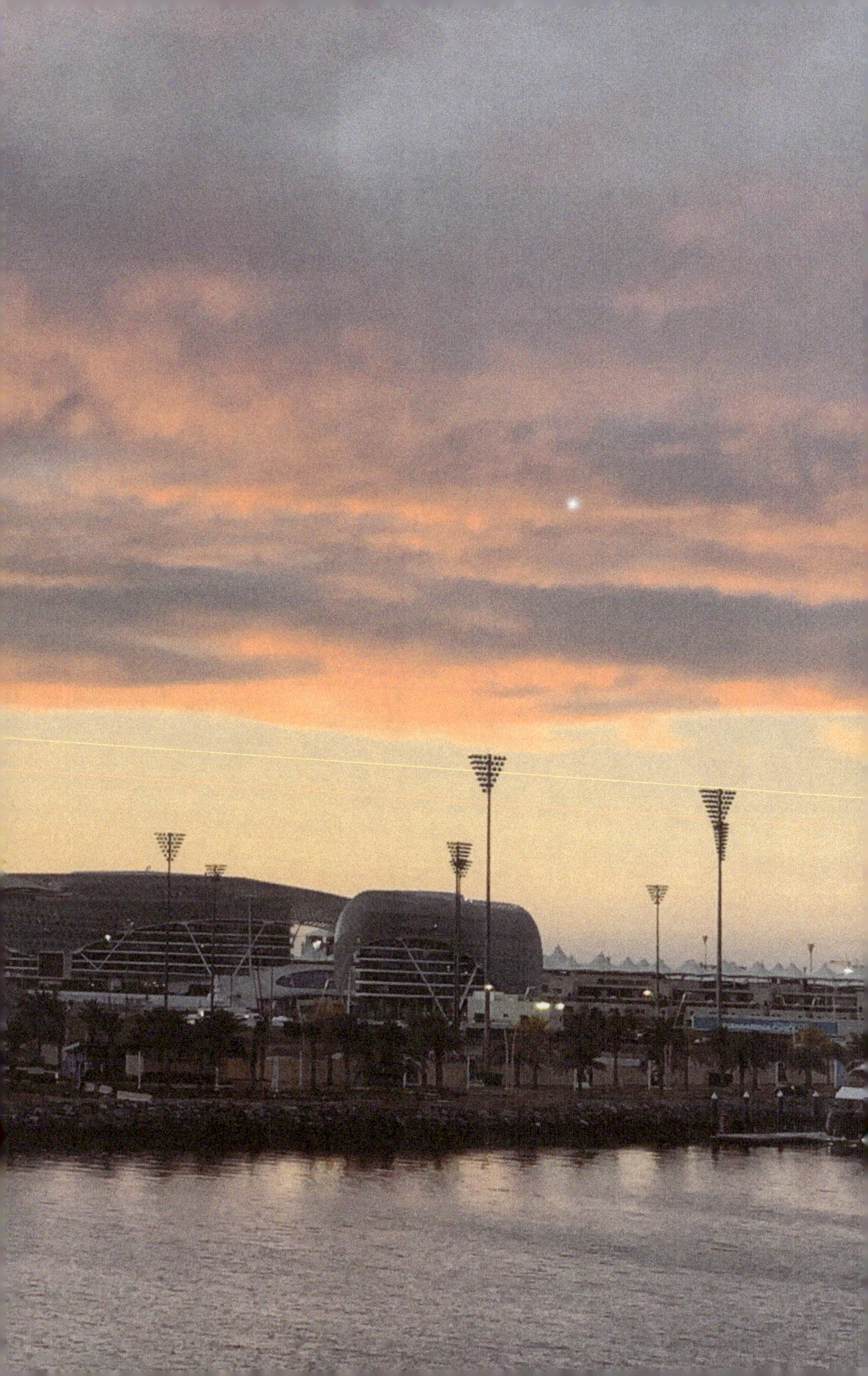

DEATH BY CHOCOLATE MARTINI

3 oz Baileys Irish Cream

1 oz premium chocolate liqueur

1 oz premium vodka

Chocolate syrup

Something chocolate to garnish (shavings, sprinkles, mini M&Ms, etc.)

Pour Baileys Irish Cream, chocolate liqueur, and vodka into a cocktail shaker half filled with ice. Shake vigorously until well chilled. Drizzle chocolate syrup into a martini glass and immediately pour in the drink. Garnish with chocolate.

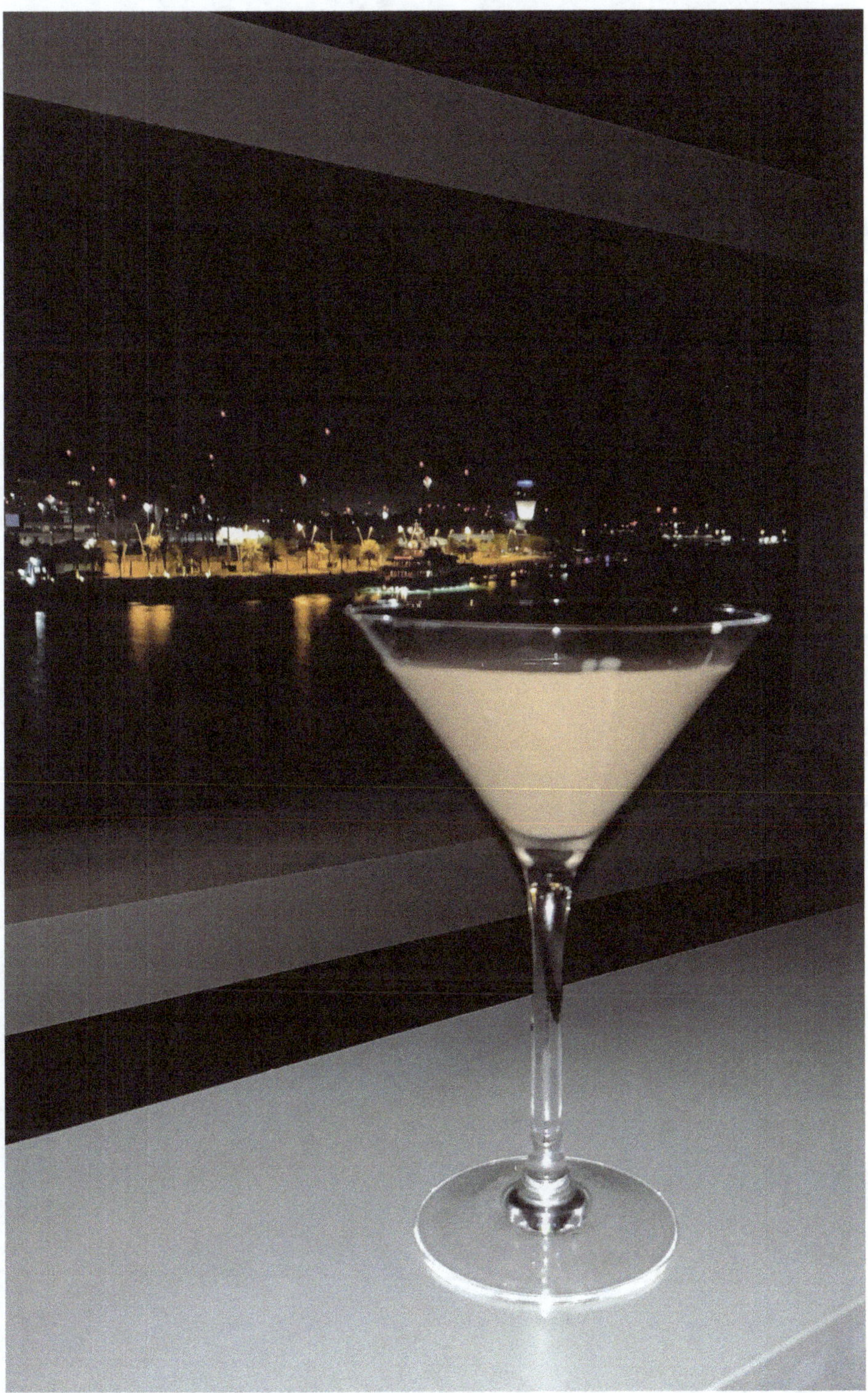

SEA BREEZE

3 oz vodka

6 oz cranberry juice

3 oz grapefruit juice

Lime wheels to garnish

Pour vodka, cranberry juice and grapefruit juice into a large pitcher and stir well to mix. Pour over ice in a tall glass and garnish with lime wheel. You can also freeze lime wedges and drop into glass as garnish in place of lime wheel.

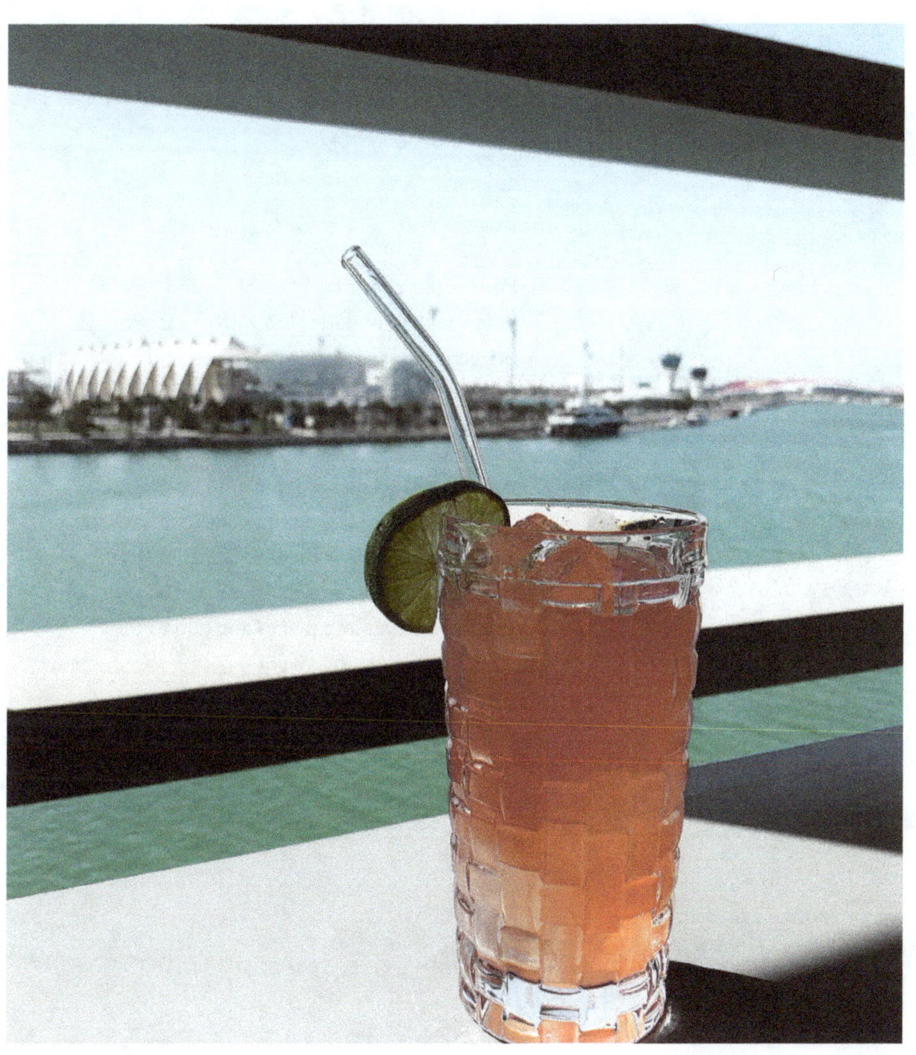

BOOZY BALCONY LEMONADE

2 oz vodka

4 oz basil lemonade

Club soda

Lemon slices and basil
  leaves for garnish

~~~~~~~~~~~~~~~~~~~~~~~~~~~~~~~~~~~

Lemonade

1 ¼ cup sugar

1 cup + 7 cups water

1 ½ cup fresh squeezed
  lemon juice

10-15 fresh basil leaves

Pour vodka over a tall glass of ice and follow with lemonade. Top with club soda. Stir gently to mix. Add lemon wheel and basil leaf for garnish.

To make lemonade, place sugar and 1 cup of water in a saucepan over medium heat. Heat and stir until sugar is completely dissolved. In a large pitcher stir together sugar mixture, lemon juice and remaining 7 cups of water. Tear basil leaves into pieces and add to the lemonade. Let sit overnight.
~~~~~~~~~~~~~~~~~~~~~~~~~~~~~~~~~~~

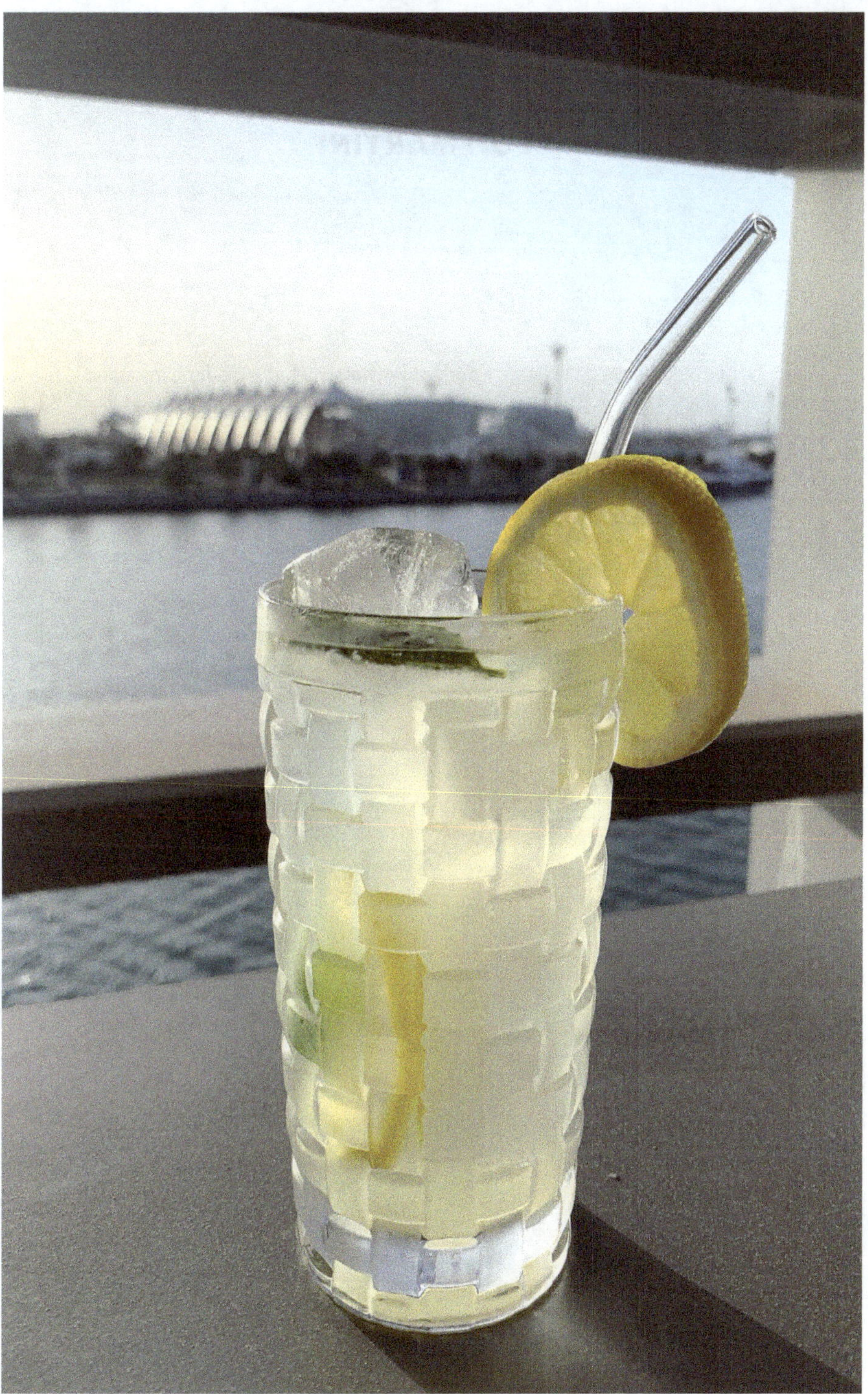

BASIL WATERMELON MARTINI

2 oz premium vodka

2 oz fresh watermelon juice

Squeeze of fresh lime juice

3-4 fresh basil leaves

*Honey or agave syrup
  to sweeten (optional)*

Pour vodka, watermelon juice, lime juice and honey in to cocktail shaker half filled with ice. Shake vigorously for 30 seconds and strain into a chilled martini glass. Place the fresh basil leaves in your palm and give them a good slap. Drop into drink for garnish.

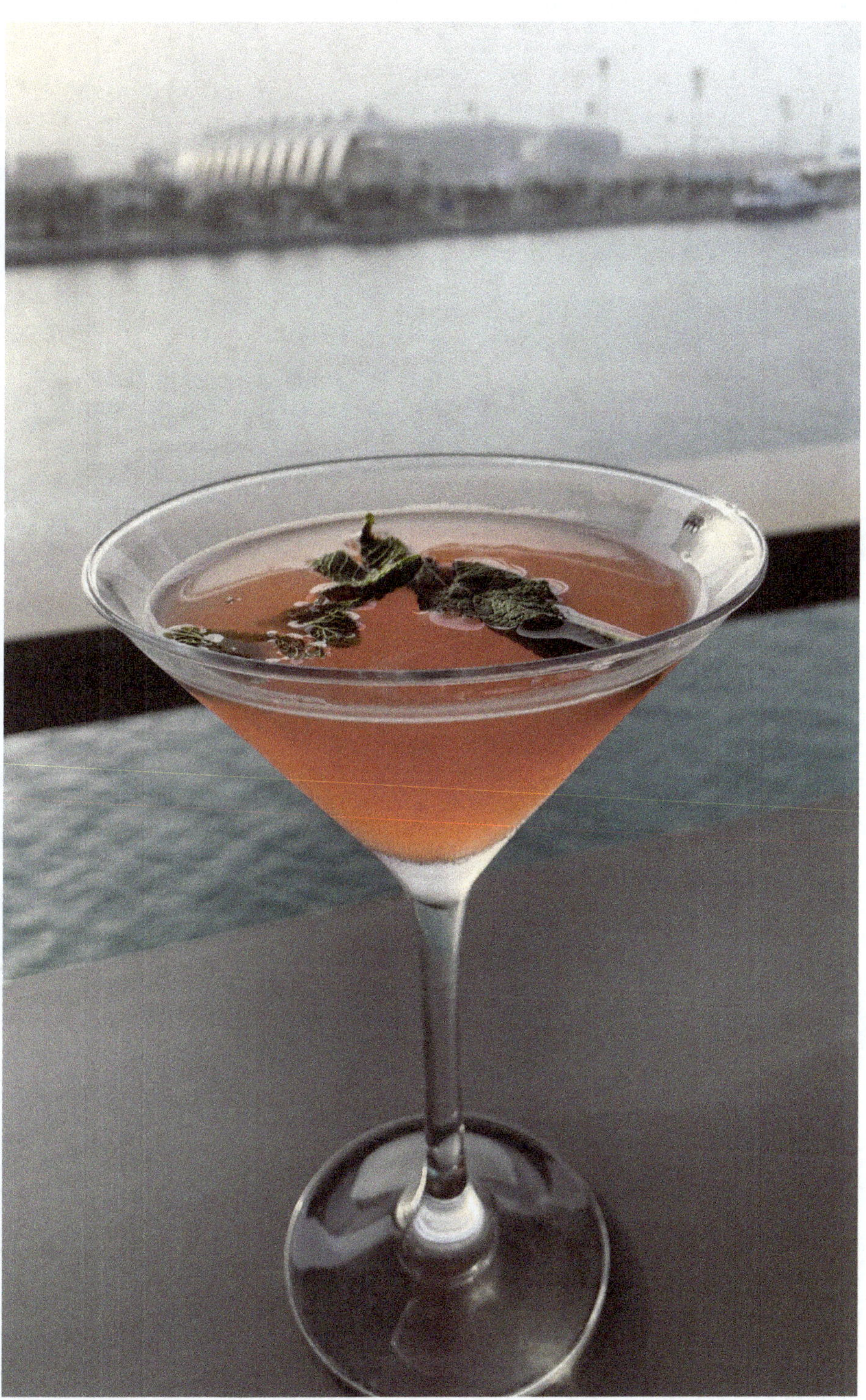

LEMON DROP MARTINI

Lemon sugar

½ cup granulated sugar

Zest from 1 lemon

Lemon Drop Martini

2 oz premium vodka

1 oz Cointreau

1 oz fresh squeezed lemon juice

¾ oz simple syrup

Pour sugar onto a plate and mix in lemon zest with your fingers until tinted yellow and fragrant. Moisten the rim of the martini glass with lemon juice and turn upside down and twist into the lemon sugar to coat the rim. Set aside

Pour vodka, Cointreau, lemon juice and simple syrup into a cocktail shaker half filled with ice. Shake for 30 seconds until well chilled. Strain into prepared martini glass and serve immediately. You can also eliminate the sugar rim and use a lemon wheel as garnish.

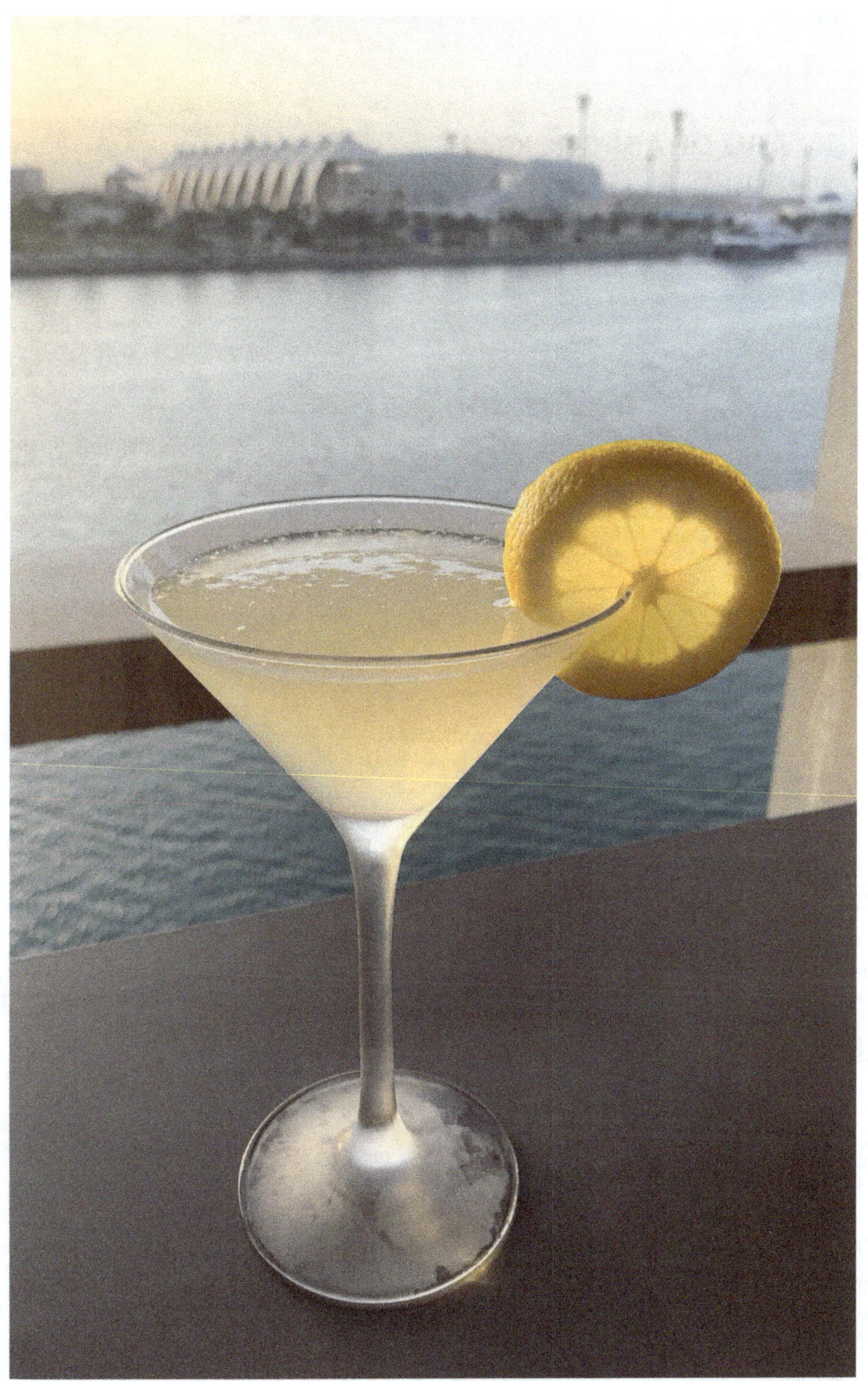

ABU DHABI COCKTAIL

1 ½ oz white rum

1 ½ oz grapefruit juice

1 oz lime juice

2 tsps superfine sugar

Dash bitters

Lime wedge to garnish

Pour rum, grapefruit juice, lime, bitters and sugar into a cocktail shaker filled with ice. Shake for 30 seconds until well mixed and chilled. Strain into a chilled cocktail glass and garnish with a lime wedge.

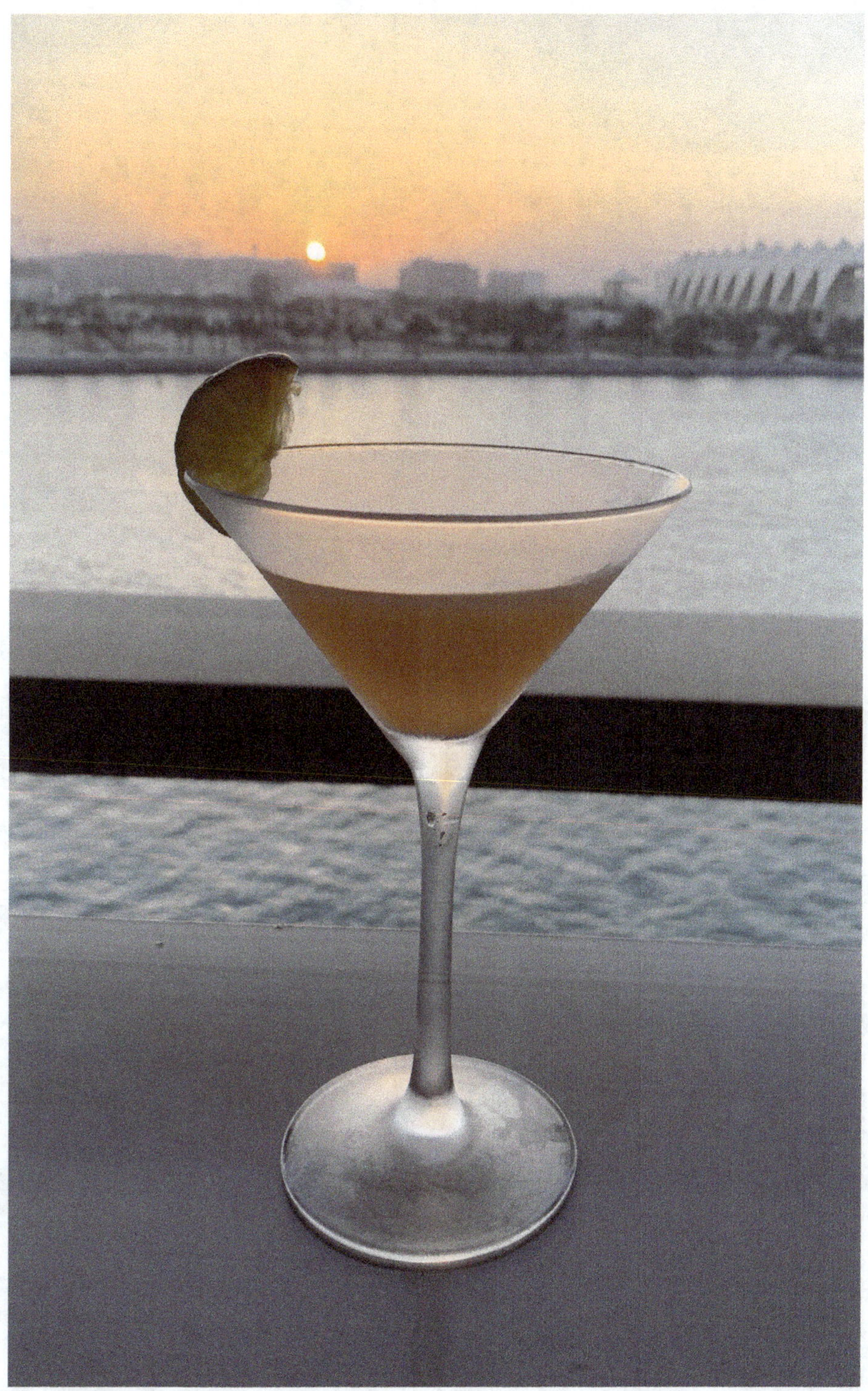

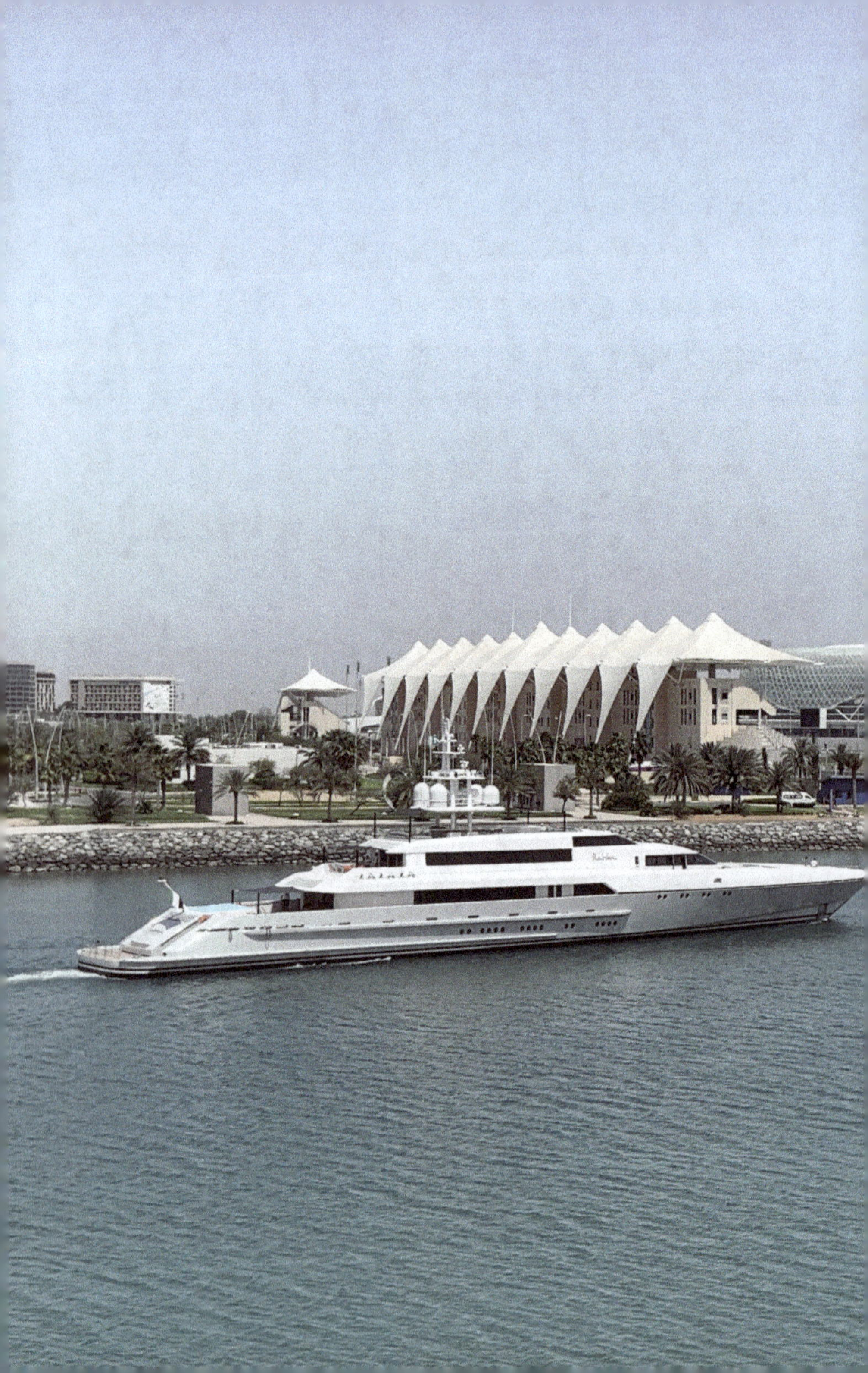

VIEW FROM MY BALCONY

Toward the end of March, I started working exclusively from home. I am very blessed to live in a spacious apartment with an open floor plan, floor to ceiling windows, a large balcony and overlooking the water. My office, is a small desk, nestled in the corner of my living/dining room so I can look out over the balcony and the water.

Most days, the water is beautiful shades of aqua, turquoise and teal. It ripples gently along the stone sides of the canal and the subtle movement of the water provides a relaxing backdrop to the endless web meetings, conference calls and emails. Boats of all shapes and sizes glide up and down, darting in or out of the nearby marina. Massive private yachts sit moored across the canal longing for the days when people were bustling around the marina. Boat traffic has slowed to a crawl since this started. The occasional jet ski races up and down making as much noise as possible to remind me there is still life outside my apartment! On special days, I can see fish in large schools swimming and jumping and making it seem like the ocean is literally boiling. I love the sound of them smacking the surface of the water, applauding the incredible wonder of the world around us.

I am in the flight path for almost every type of aircraft departing or arriving at Abu Dhabi International Airport. It used to be a very busy airport and the planes rarely took a break. Some might be annoyed by the roar of an A-380 as it buzzes seemingly through your living room. I love it – love watching the planes and hearing that noise and thinking about the possibilities of the people on the plane. I have an app on my mobile phone that lets me track the planes as I sit on my balcony. I know the types of aircraft by sight now and usually by sound. I am fascinated by the ability of such a heavy piece of machinery soaring through the sky as effortlessly as the sea birds. I long to go to all the places those planes go and wish I could see every sight they have seen gliding over water, land and sea.

Yas Marina, Yas Marina Circuit and Ferrari
World sit directly across from me. These
usually provide hours of entertainment as
I watch the hustle bustle of traffic coming
and going, hear the never-ending roar of
race cars going around the track or watch
the lights and music bouncing out of the bars
and restaurants. There has been nothing but
deafening silence now for months. The track
and adjoining hotel are closed since the first
part of March when a bicycle race team that
was staying at the hotel had a couple of their
team test positive for COVID. Bars were one
of the first public places to close, followed
shortly after by restaurants and other public
places like amusement parks.

The beautiful view of the water, the
interesting, albeit quiet, buildings have
made working from home a dream. Being
able to sit on my balcony and feel the soft
breeze from the water tickle my face while
I have my morning coffee is simply heaven.
Being still with nowhere to rush off to,
listening to the music of birds singing and
the fish dancing give me plenty of space
to reflect on what really matters. What is
really my purpose? Will life return to what
I knew before COVID? When? How? Will
I get sick? Will my friends or family get
sick? How long will this last? So many
unanswered questions....and a quarantini
on the balcony to sip as I ponder.

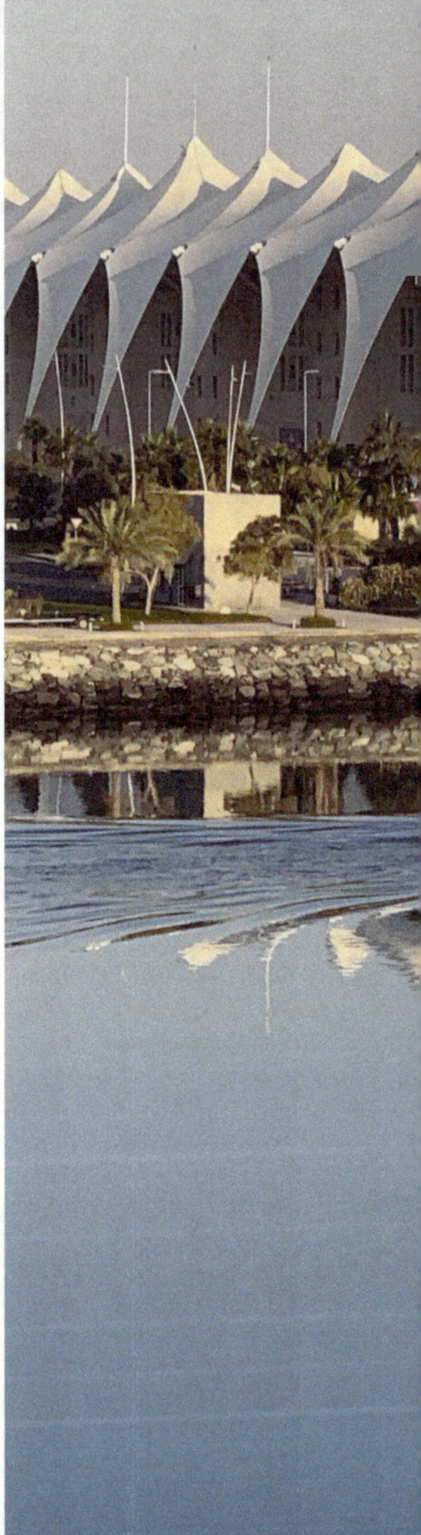

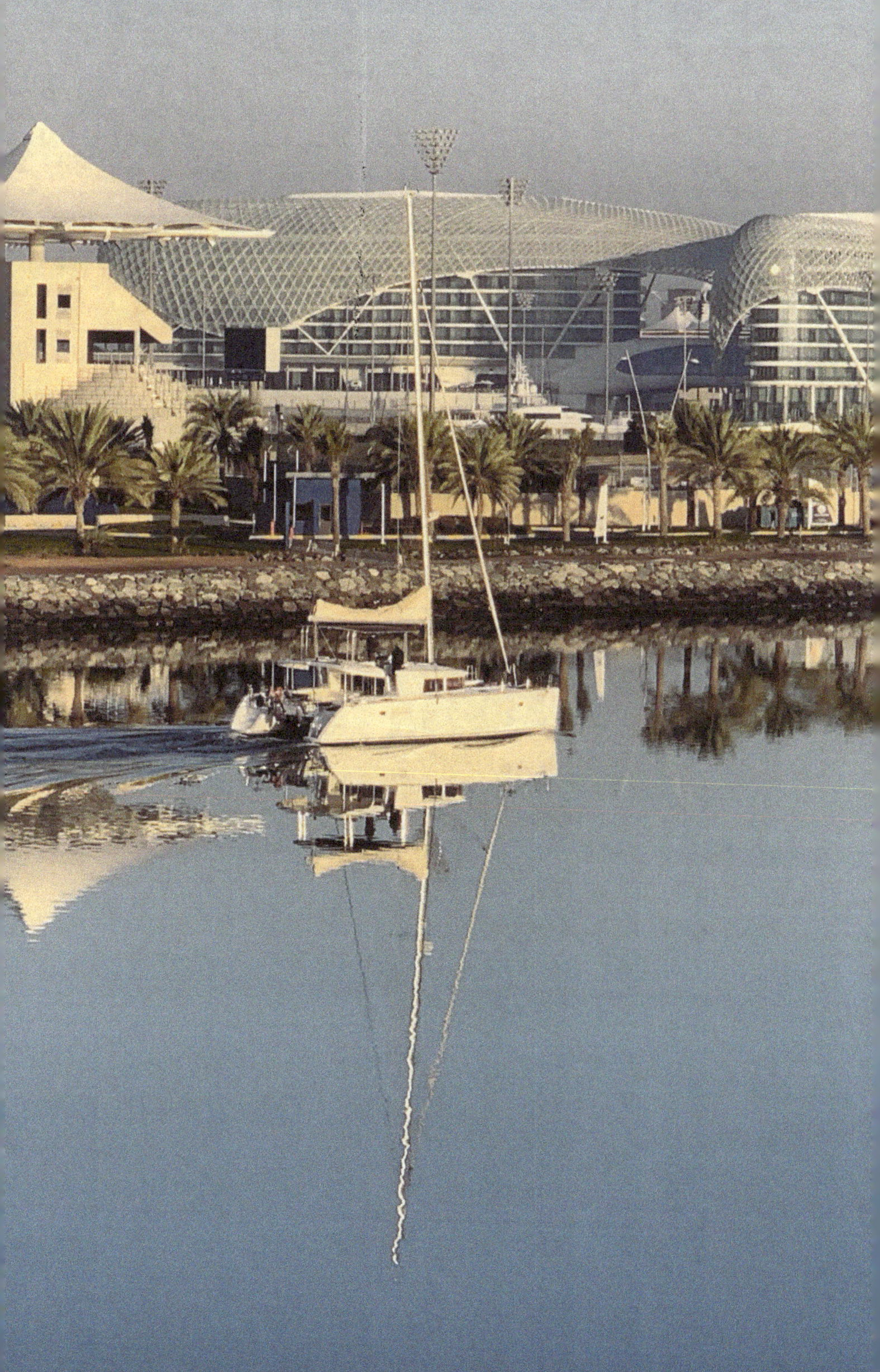

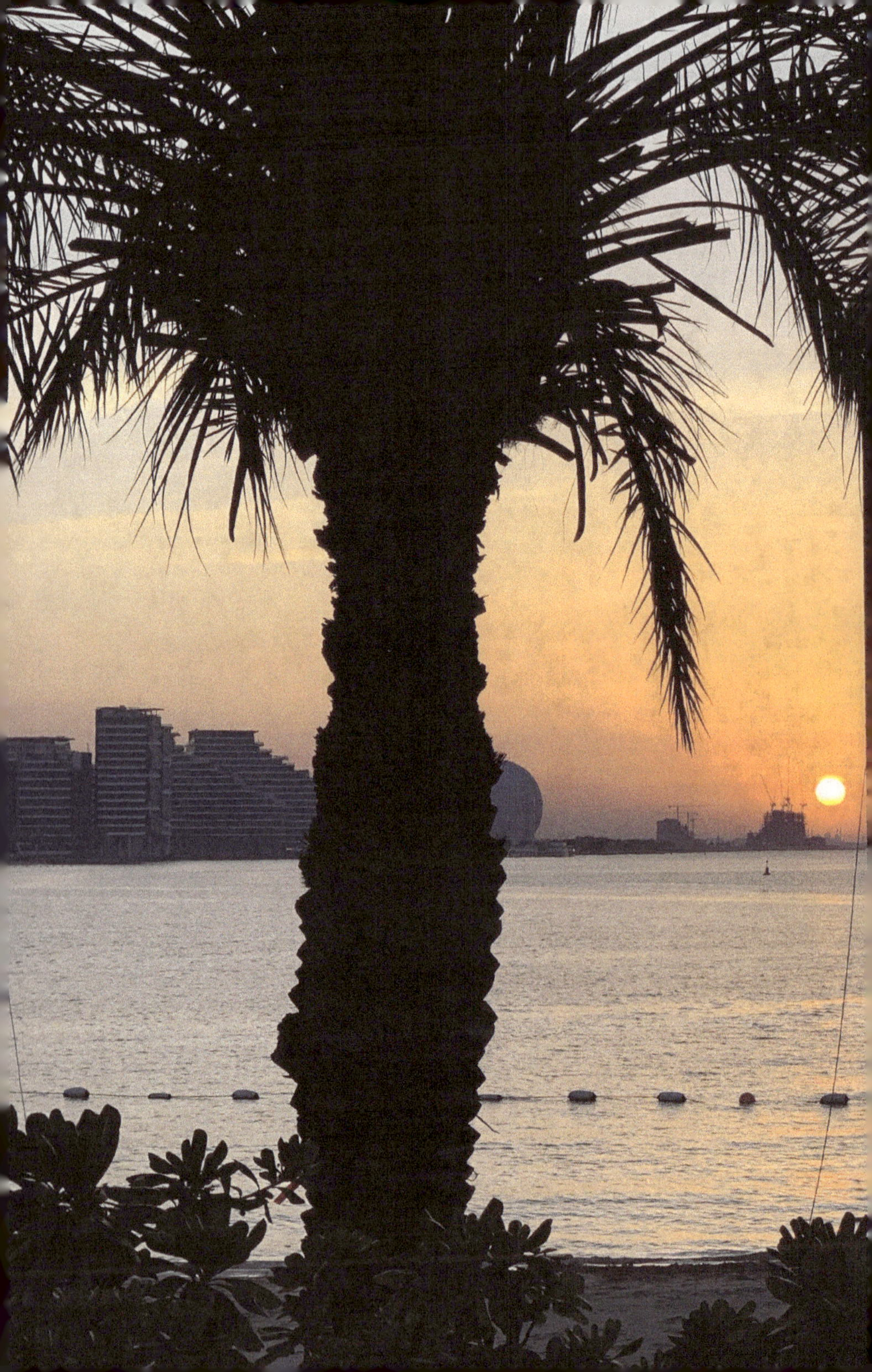

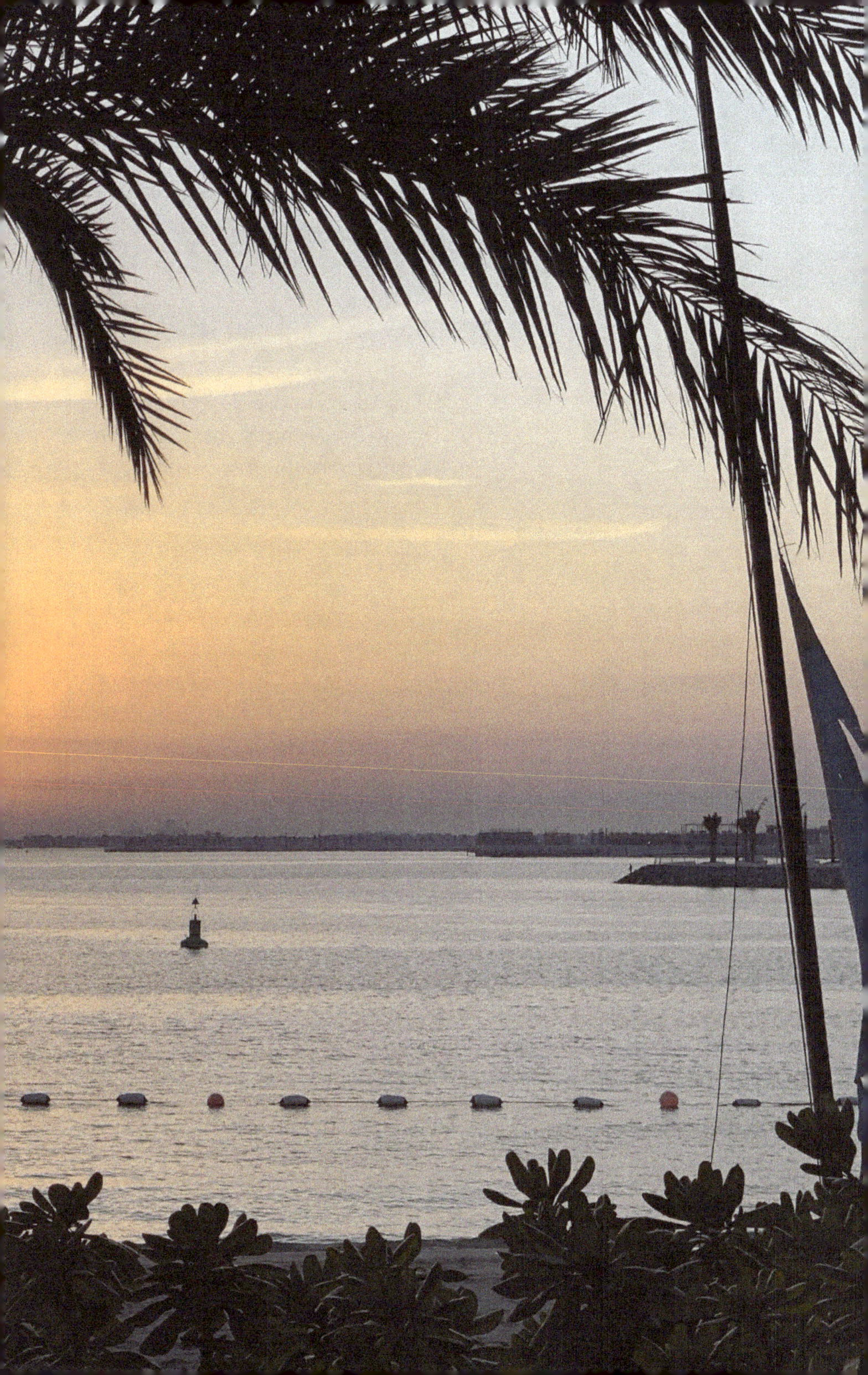

PINA COLADA

3 oz fresh frozen pineapple
  chunks – about seven
  1-inch chunks

3 oz coconut rum
  (white rum works fine too)

1.5 oz coconut cream

10 small ice cubes

1 tsp lime juice (optional)

Add all ingredients to a blender and pulse until smooth. Pour into a tall glass and garnish with a fresh pineapple wedge.

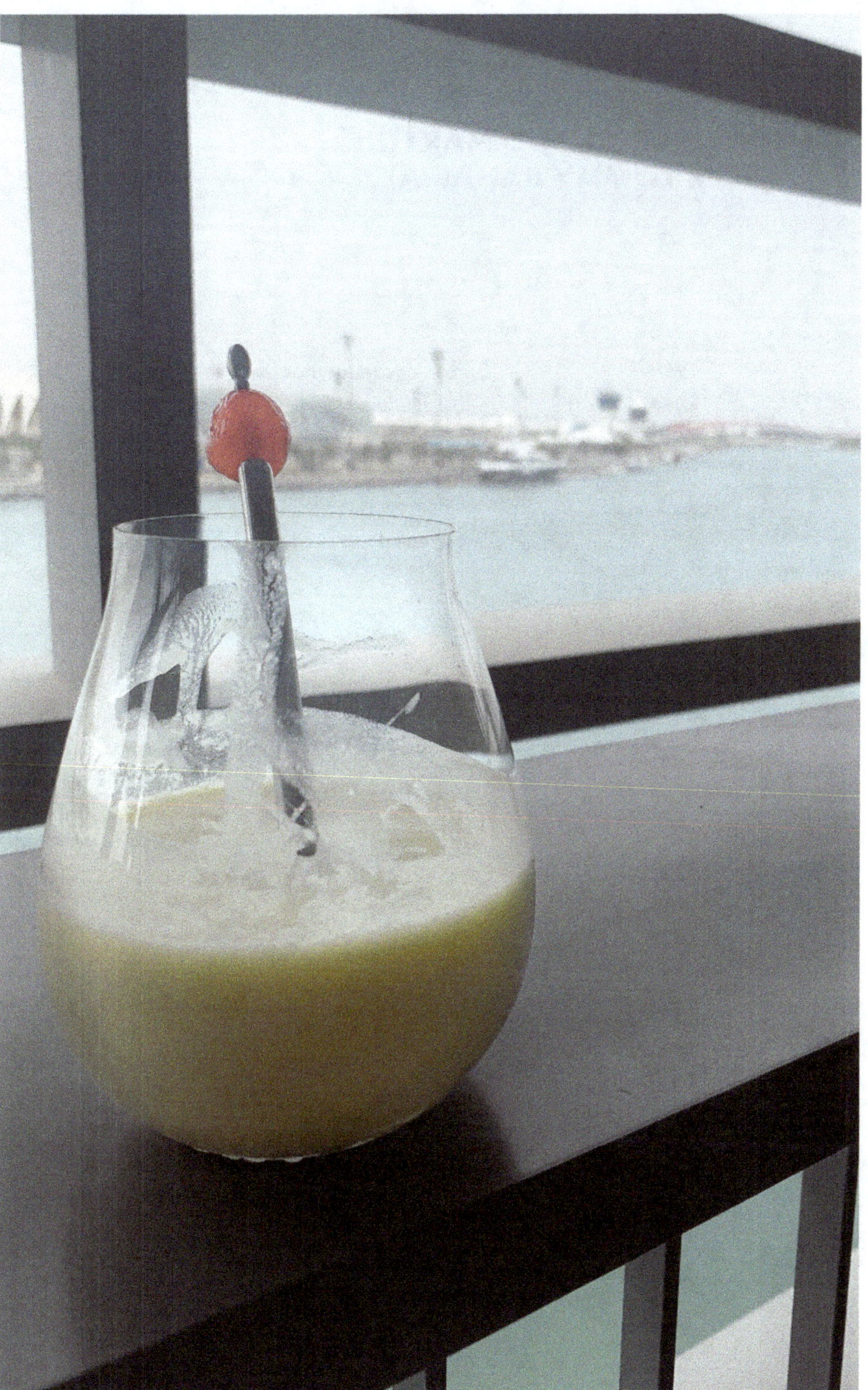

COCONUT CLOUD MARTINI (FROM TOMMY BAHAMA)

Toasted Coconut

Honey

1 oz good white rum

1.5 oz coconut rum

½ oz crème of coconut

1.5 oz vanilla vodka

Spread coconut onto baking sheet and put into 320-degree oven until toasted golden brown. Allow to cool. Pour a small amount of honey on a plate and turn martini glass upside down and dip slightly into honey and then into toasted coconut to coat rim.

Pour rum, coconut rum, crème of coconut and vanilla vodka into cocktail shaker half filled with ice. Shake for 20 seconds until well chilled and strain immediately into prepared martini glass.

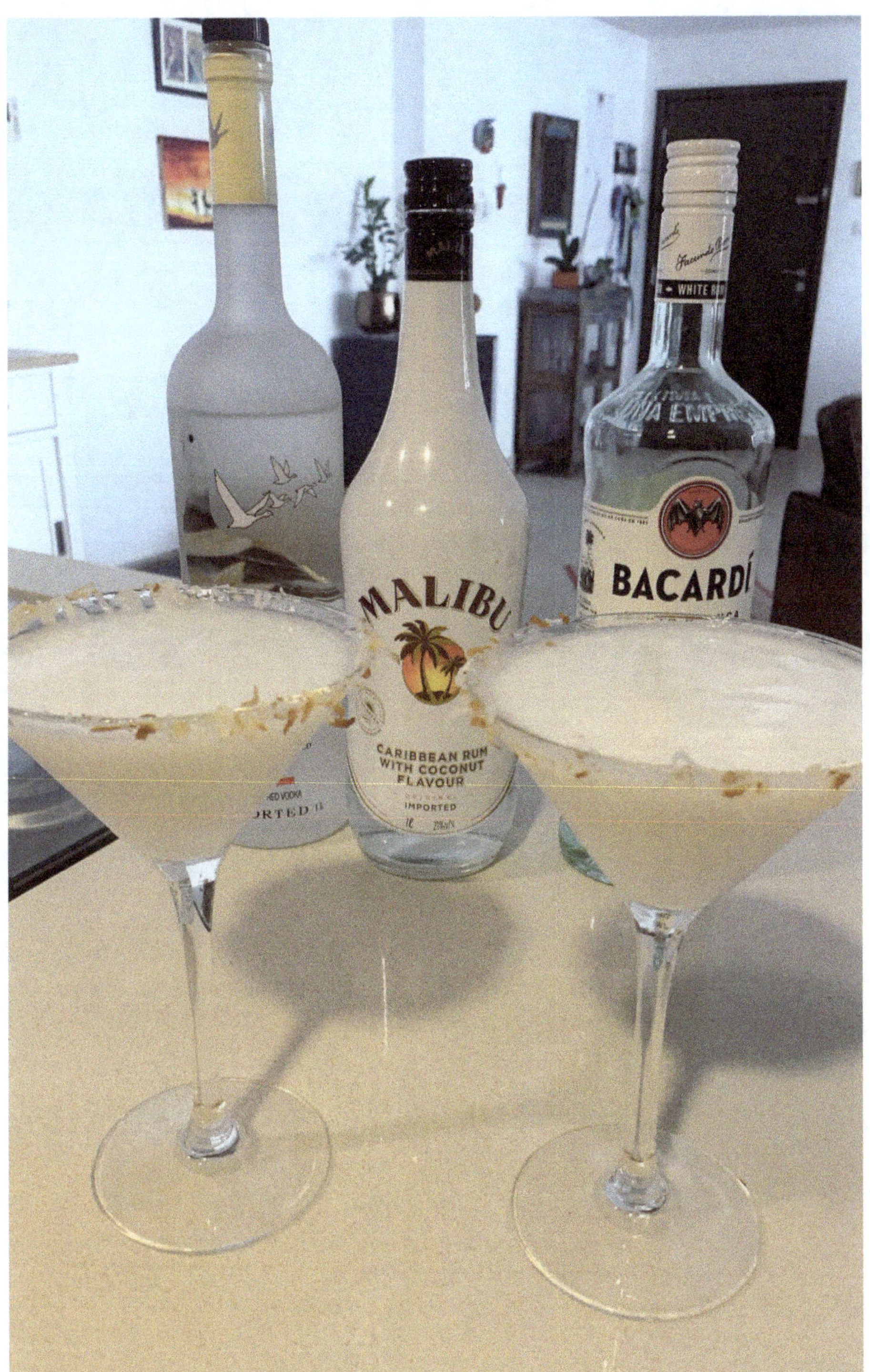

MALIBU
CARIBBEAN RUM
WITH COCONUT
FLAVOUR
IMPORTED
BACARDÍ

CLASSIC MOJITO

1 lime

1 tsp granulated sugar

Small handful of
* fresh mint leaves*

2 oz good white rum

Soda water
* (can use lime soda*
* for added sweetness)*

Cut half the lime into small pieces, reserve the other half for garnish. Put lime pieces, sugar, and mint leaves in a tall glass and muddle together. Add rum and stir to mix well. Fill the glass with crushed ice and top off with club soda. Garnish with a fresh mint sprig and lime wedge.

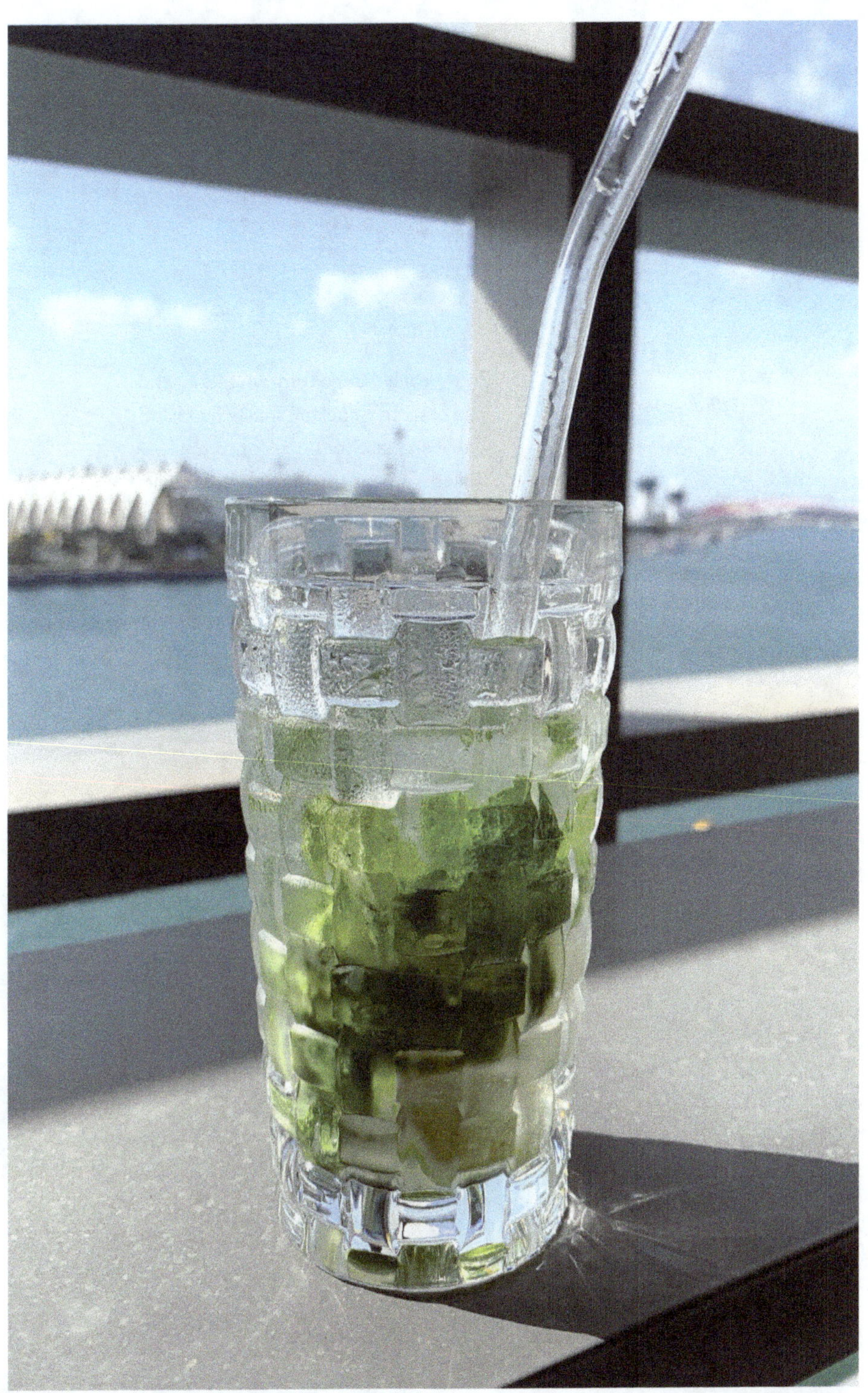

MANGO PEACH TEA MARTINI

2 oz Pritchard's Peach
Mango Rum

1 oz good white rum

2 oz peach flavored
iced tea

2-3 mint leaves
for garnish

Pour peach mango rum, white rum and iced tea into a cocktail shaker half filled with ice. Shake for 20 seconds until chilled. Strain immediately into a chilled martini glass. Put mint leaves in the palm of one hand and give them a good smack. Drop into drink and enjoy.

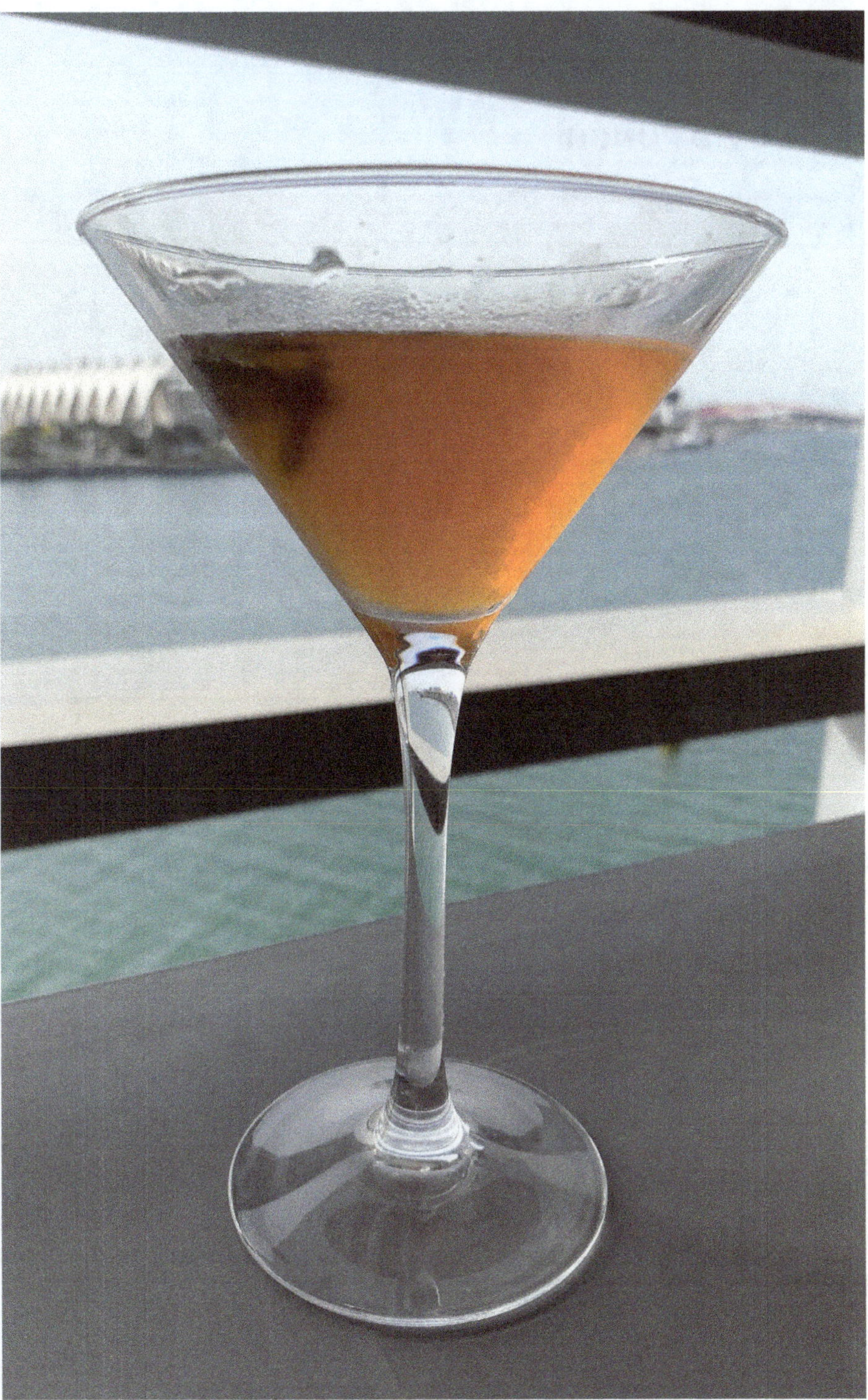

COVID PUNCH

½ cup light-brown sugar

½ cup water

½ cup packed fresh
  mint leaves, plus sprig
  for garnish

1 ½ cups fresh orange juice

¾ cup fresh lime juice

5 oz white rum

Combine brown sugar and water in a saucepan and bring to a boil over medium-high heat, stirring once. Remove from heat and add mint leaves. Let steep for 10 minutes. Remove leaves and let cool.

Stir together orange juice, lime juice, rum and ¾ cup of syrup in a pitcher. Pour into tall glasses filled with ice and garnish with a fresh mint sprig.

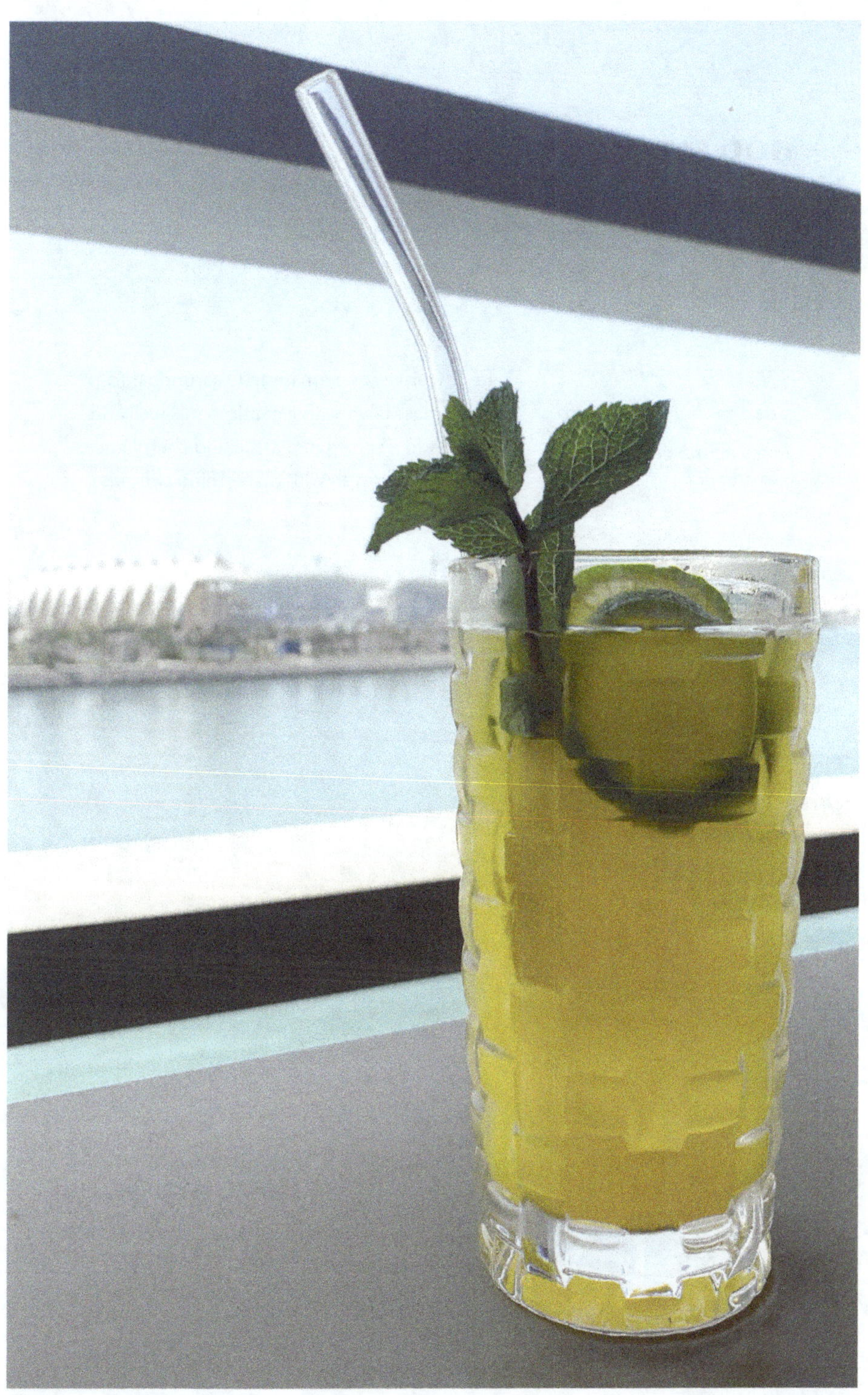

GOD FATHER

2 oz premium whiskey

2 oz amaretto Disaronno

Maraschino cherries
   to garnish

Pour whiskey and amaretto Disaronno into rocks glass filled with ice. Stir to mix well and chill. Add a splash of maraschino cherry juice if desires. Garnish with maraschino cherries.

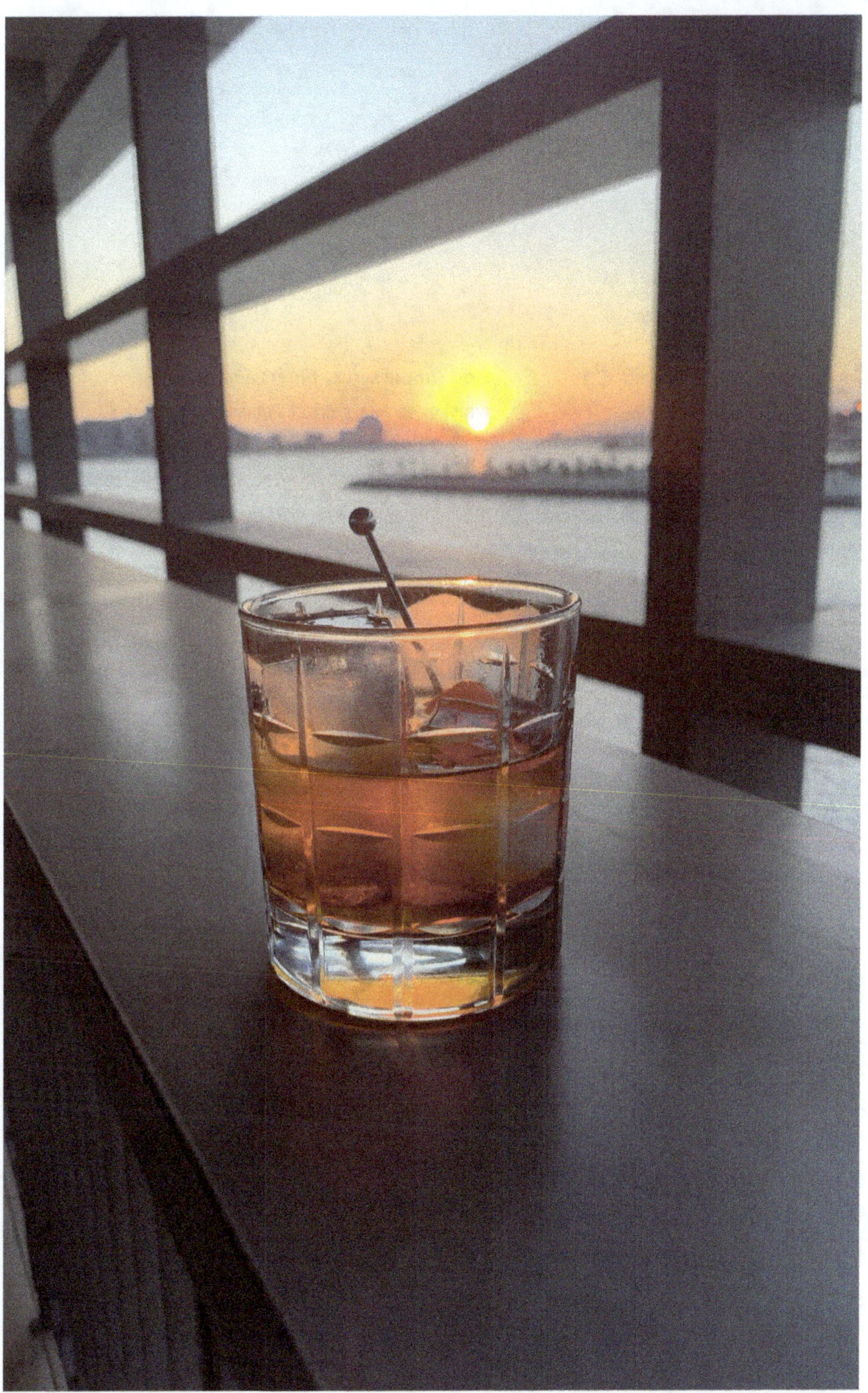

OLD FASHIONED

*1.5 oz premium bourbon
 or whiskey*

2 bar spoons of simple syrup

3 dashes Angostura Bitters

Orange peel

*Maraschino cherry
 (optional)*

Add simple syrup, bitters and bourbon or whiskey to a large rocks glass. Add ice and stir gently until the ice and the liquid equalize. Zest and orange peel over the glass and drop into drink. Add maraschino cherry if desired.

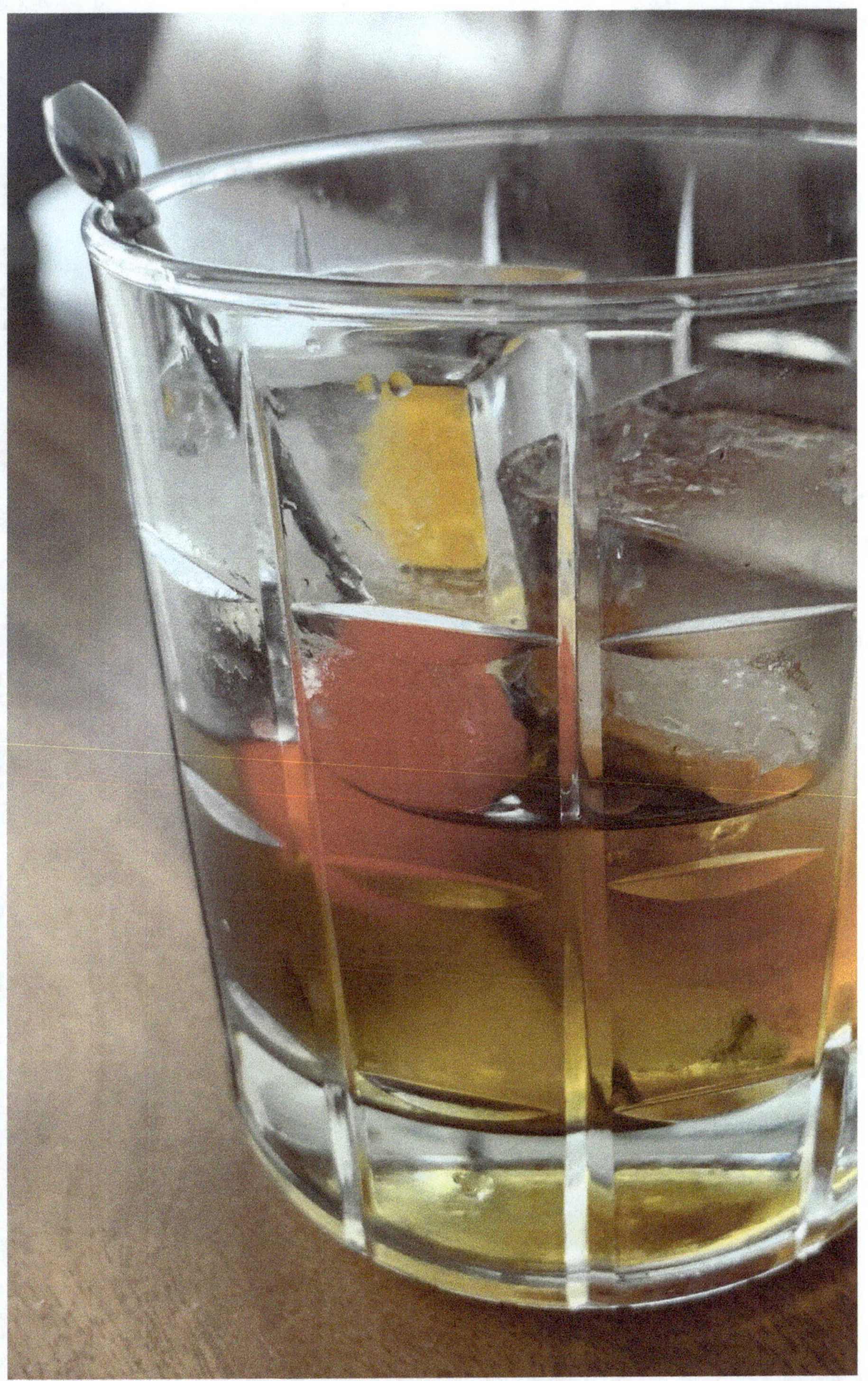

BLUSHING BETSY
(COURTESY OF THE PIONEER WOMAN)

½ grapefruit

2 oz whiskey

2 rough cut sugar cubes

Put sugar cubes into large rocks glass and pour in whiskey. Muddle to dissolve sugar cubes. Use vegetable peeler to peel a large strip of grapefruit and twist over drink. Drop peel into glass, fill with ice and top with juice from ½ grapefruit.

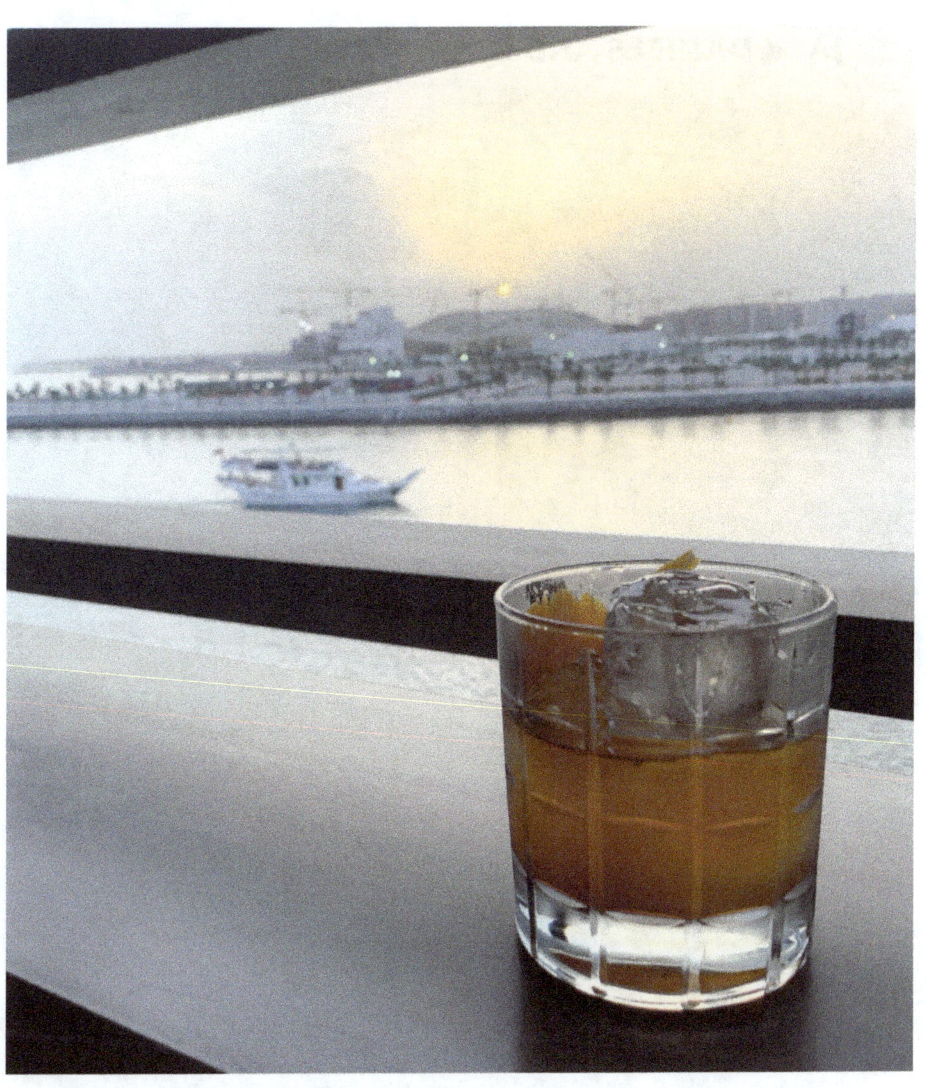

JACK DANIELS AND GINGER ALE

2 oz Jack Daniels

4 oz ginger ale

Fill a large rocks glass with ice. Pour in Jack Daniels and top with ginger ale.

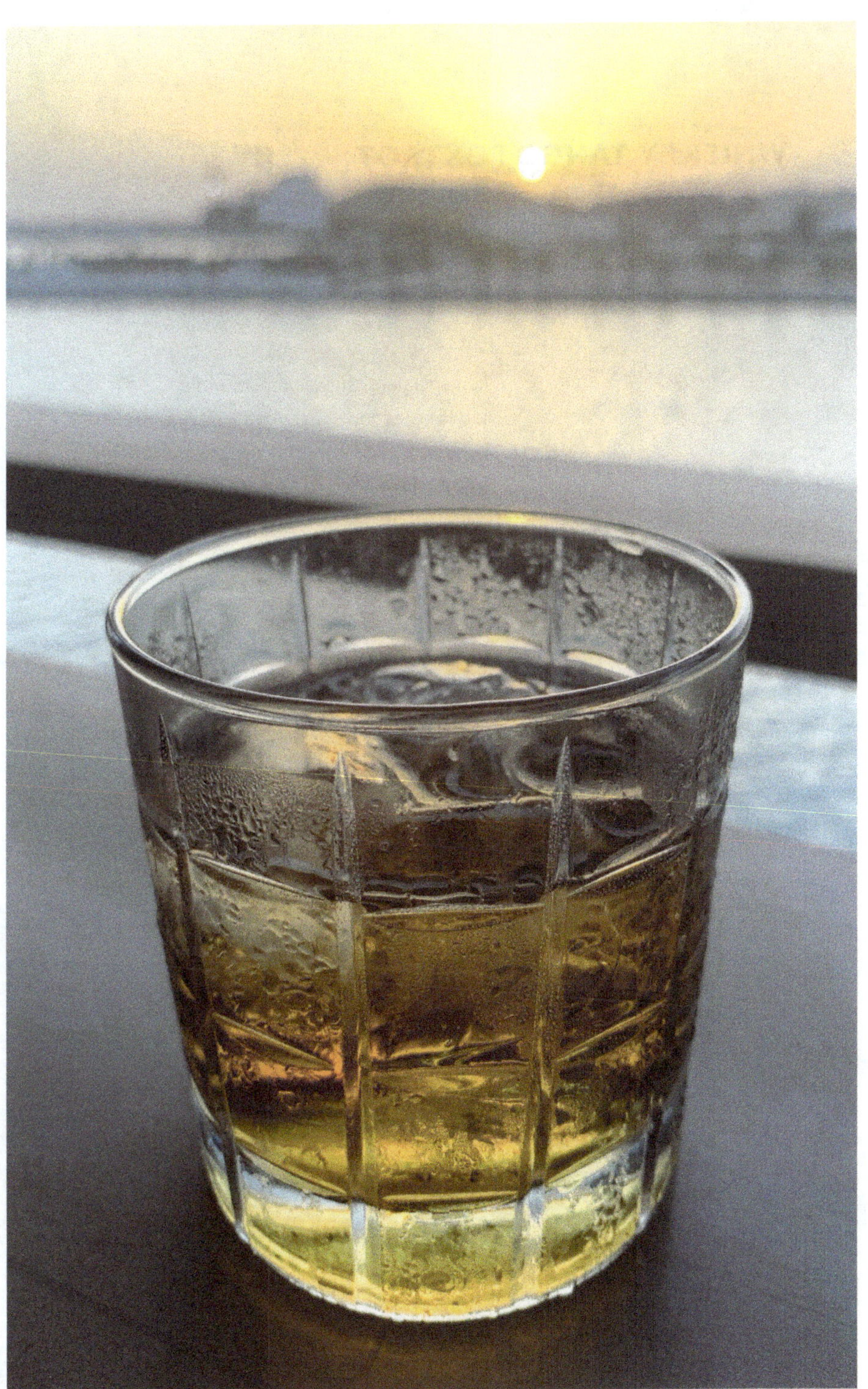

WHISKEY TANGO FOXTROT

¼ c blueberries

4 basil leaves

1 oz lemon juice

1 tsp sugar

2 oz bourbon

4 oz vermouth

4 oz soda water

In a cocktail shaker, lightly muddle blueberries and sugar. Add lemon juice, bourbon, and vermouth and stir to combine. Strain into a large rocks glass filled with ice. Slap basil leaves over glass and drop into drink. Top off with soda water.

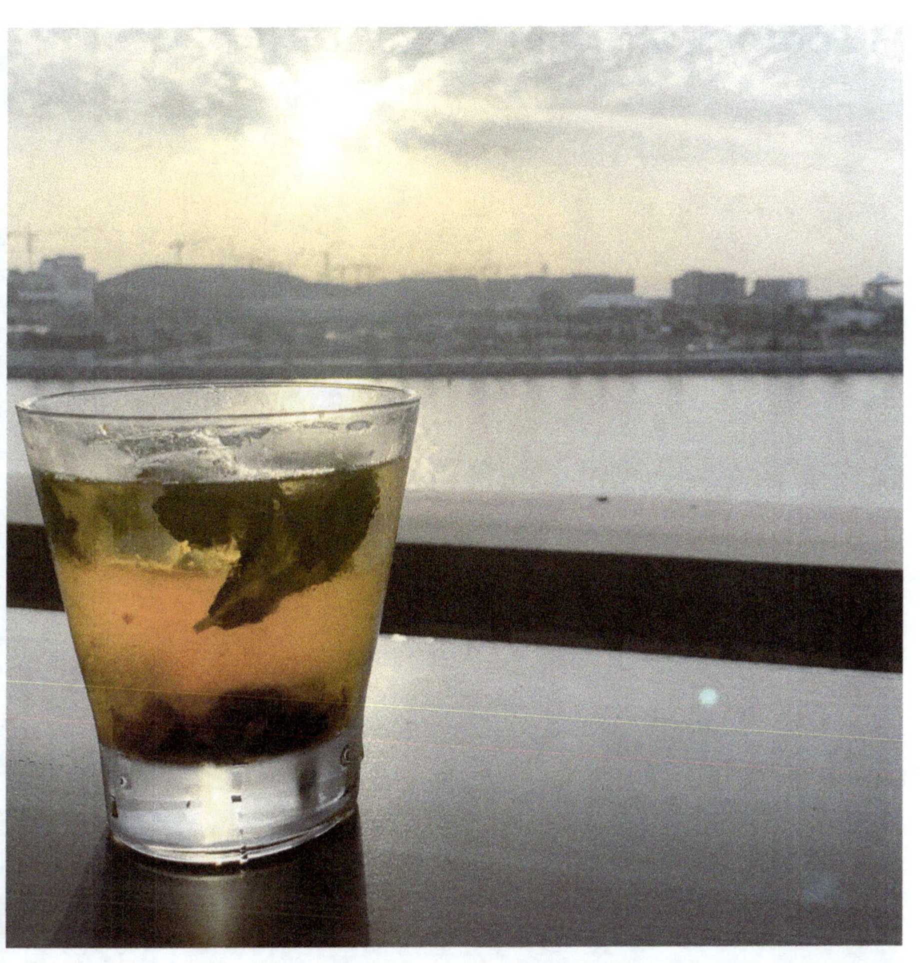

GOLDEN PINEAPPLE MARGARITA

4 oz Patron Anejo tequila

2 oz Patron Citronage orange liqueur

1 ½ oz freshly squeezed lime juice

1 oz freshly squeezed pineapple juice

Simple syrup or agave syrup to taste

Optional:

2 lime wedges for rimming glasses and garnish

¼ c coarse see salt for rimming glasses

Pineapple wedge or chunks for garnish

Combine tequila, orange liqueur, lime juice and pineapple juice in a pitcher and stir. Add simple syrup or agave syrup to taste. Rim two glasses with lime and dip in salt to coat rim if desired. Add ice and pour in tequila mixture. Garnish with lime wedge and/or pineapple wedge.

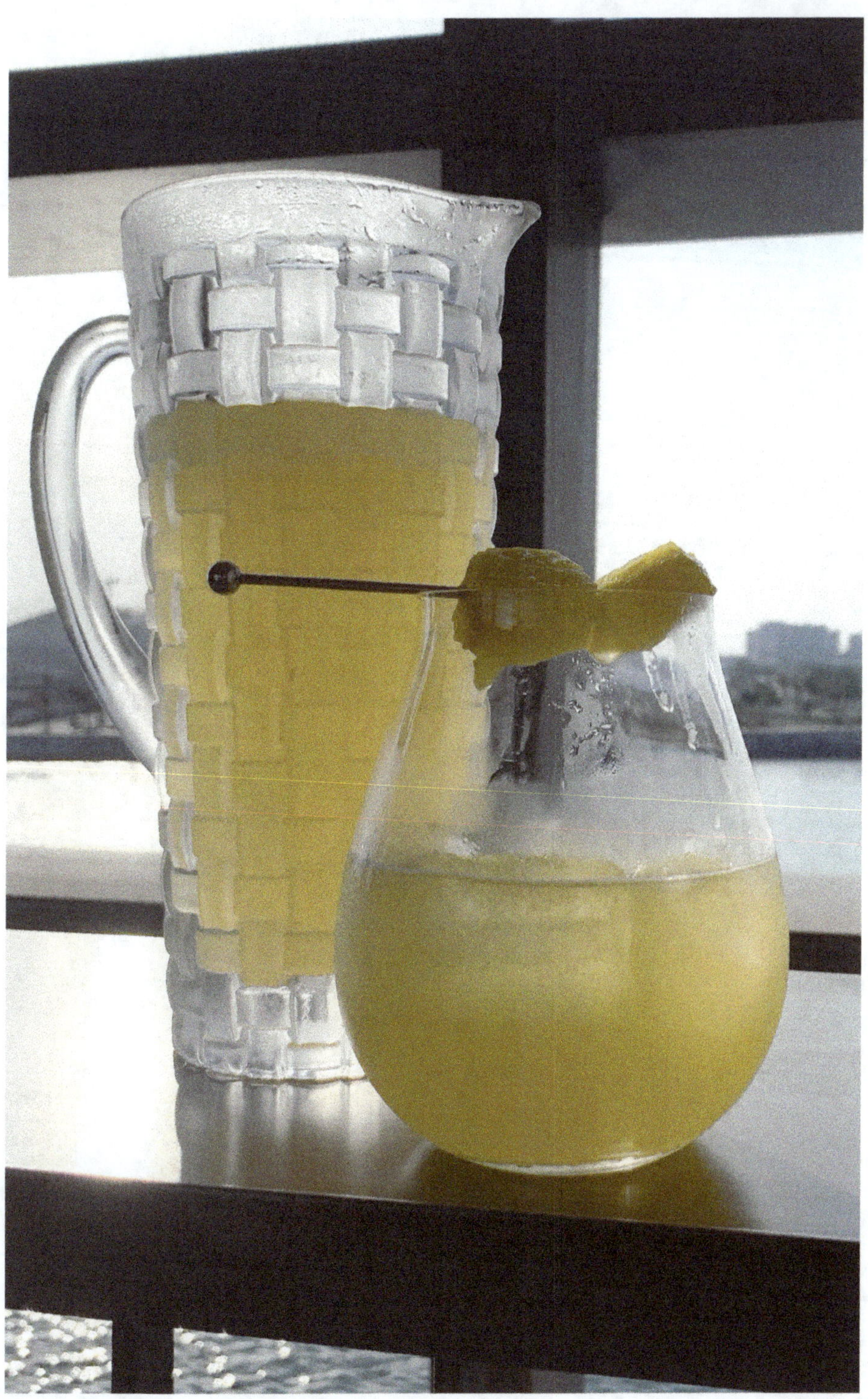

BLACKBERRY MINT JULEP

2 oz bourbon

¼ oz blackberry
  simple syrup

3-4 fresh mint leaves

Handful fresh blackberries
  for garnish

Sprig of fresh mint

Blackberry mint simple
  syrup:

1 cup fresh blackberries

8-10 fresh mint leaves

1 cup sugar

½ cup water

In a julep cup or large rocks glass, lightly muddle mint leaves and blackberry syrup. Add ice and pour in the bourbon. Stir to mix and garnish with a couple of blackberries and a sprig of fresh mint.

To make the blackberry mint simple syrup: In a small saucepan, combine blackberries, mint leaves, sugar and water over medium high heat. Bring to a boil for about 5-7 minutes. Strain through a fine mesh strainer and let cool.

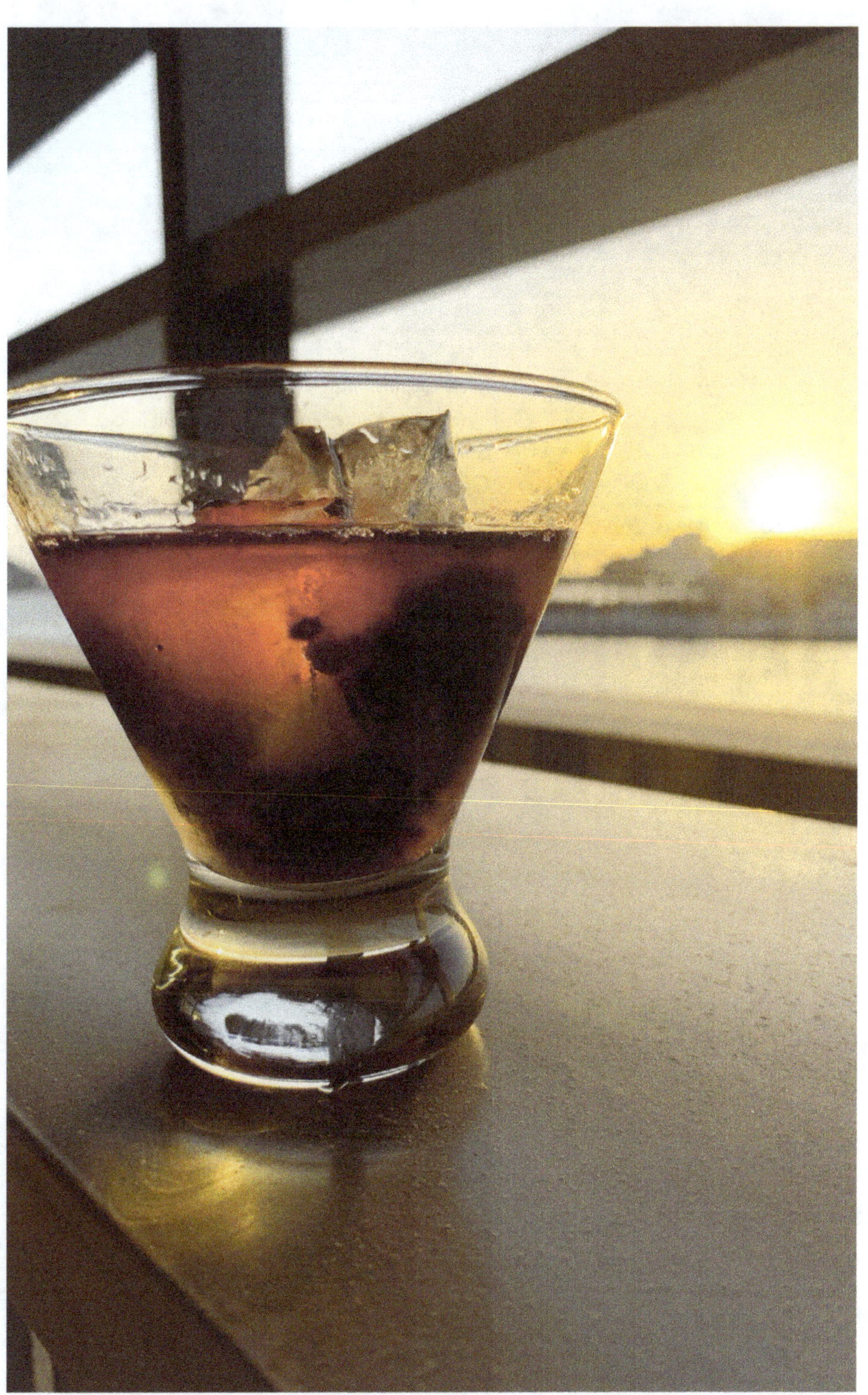

PALOMA

2 oz tequila blanco

1 tbsp fresh lime juice

2 tsp agave nectar

2 oz fresh pink
  grapefruit juice

Fever Tree Indian Tonic

Pink grapefruit wedge
  for garnish

Mint sprig for garnish

Fill a tall glass with ice and pour in tequila, lime, agave nectar and pink grapefruit juice. Stir to combine and top up with tonic water. Garnish with grapefruit wedge and/or mint sprig.

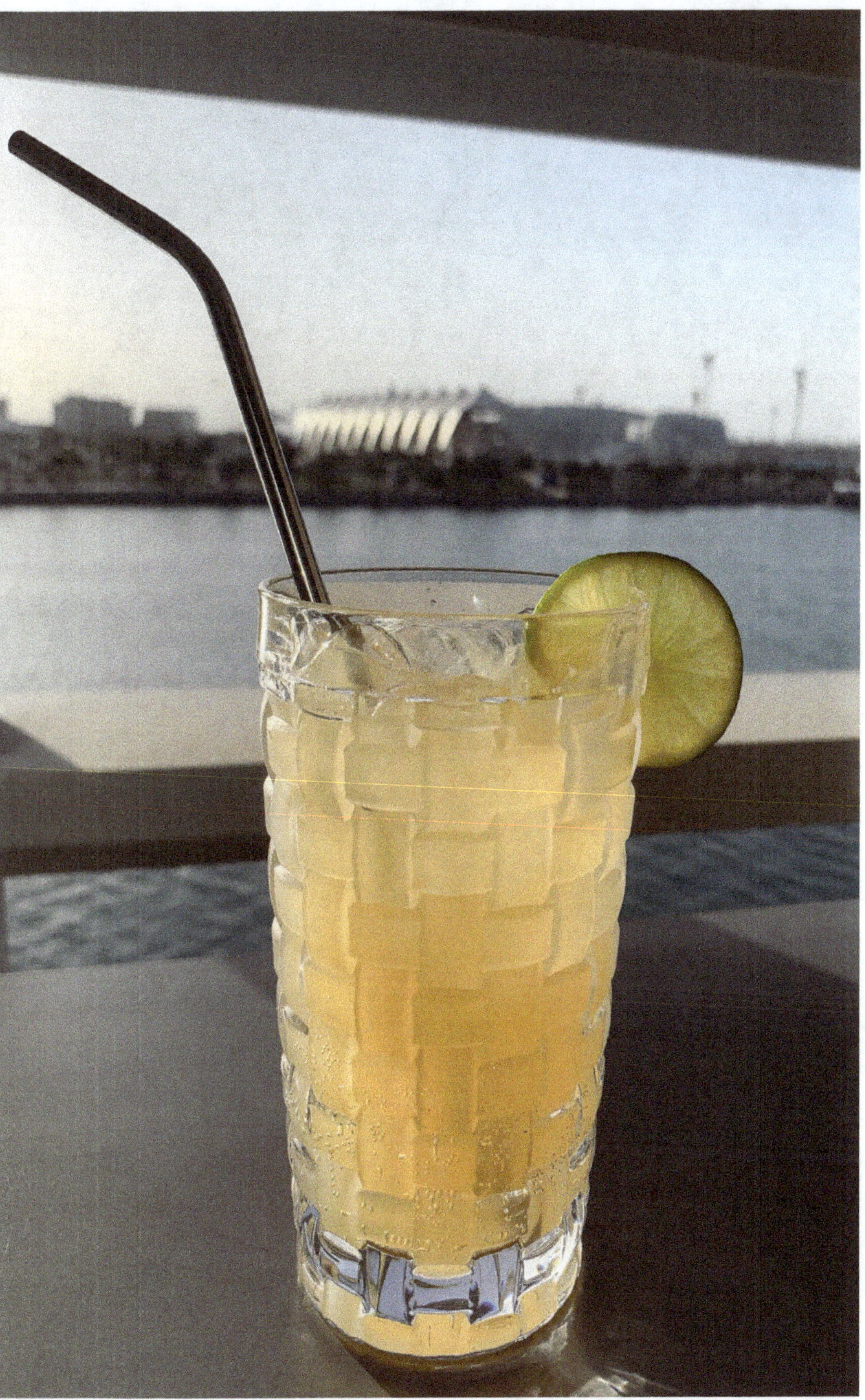

GOING HOME

This evening I went for a walk. The kind of walk you take to clear your head, to stretch your legs, to re-group. It was a perfect evening for that kind of walk. Clear cobalt blue sky with the sun shining bright orange in preparation for its nightly salute and a soft, warm breeze blowing just hard enough to keep you cool. There is a long stretch of walking pavement along the seaside that connects all of the sister residential properties on Raha Beach. Perfectly situated for a walk.

As the clutter of the day started to fall away and the smell of the sea filled my nostrils I reflected on how, in a short couple of months, life has changed dramatically. This walking path would be filled with people skating, riding bikes, walking, running, walking dogs, sitting with friends, and just generally hanging out. The beaches would be crowded with swimmers and sunbathers and picnics. Playgrounds hosting a perfectly composed symphony of children laughing and playing. But tonight, the beaches are empty and show signs that no one has been on them for weeks. Playgrounds are empty with padlocks and ropes keeping the children out. People are out, in sparse, small groups sticking to their identified cluster and giving everyone else a wide berth. Some are wearing masks, some are not. All are keeping their distance from the unknown.

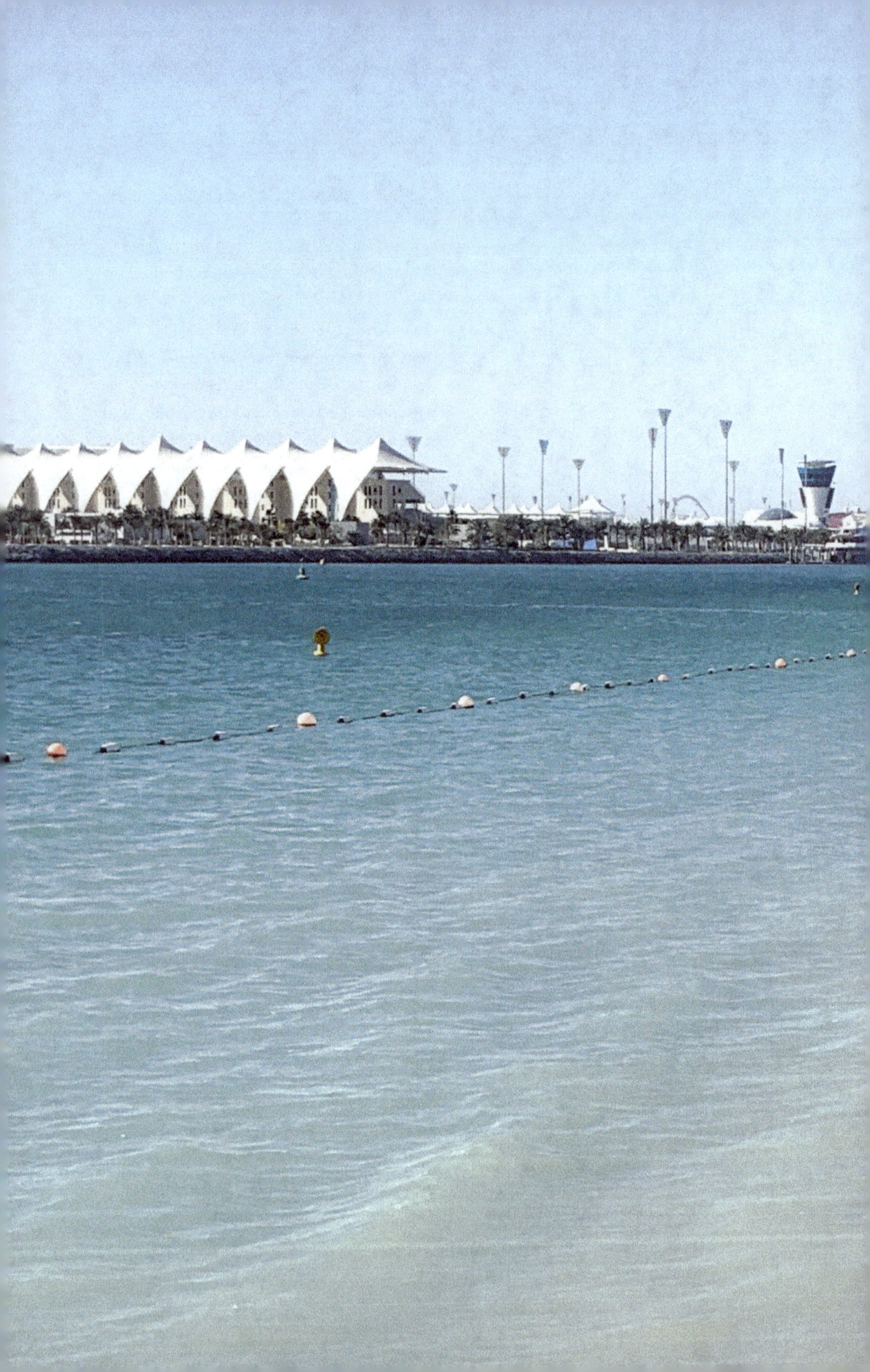

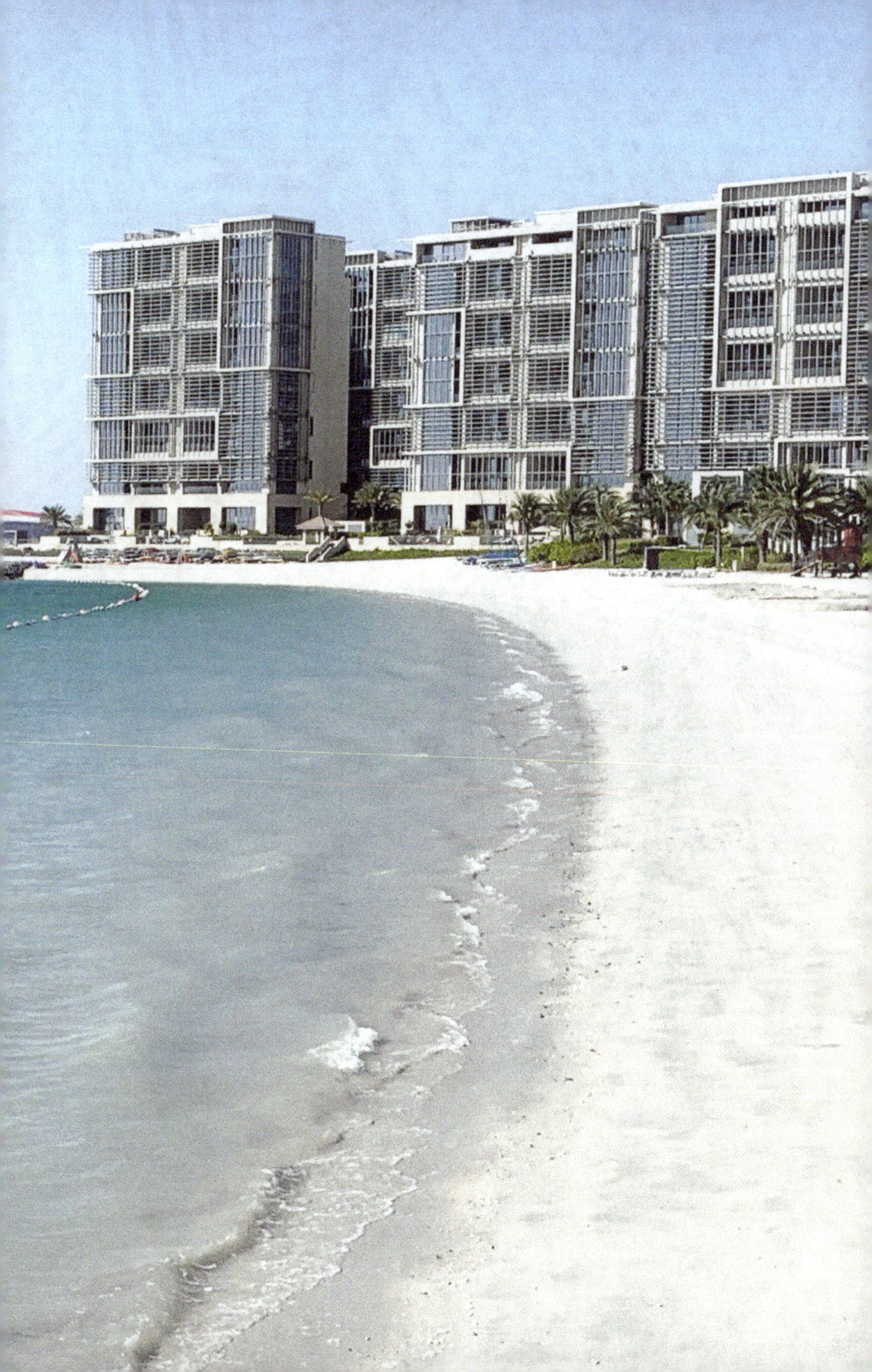

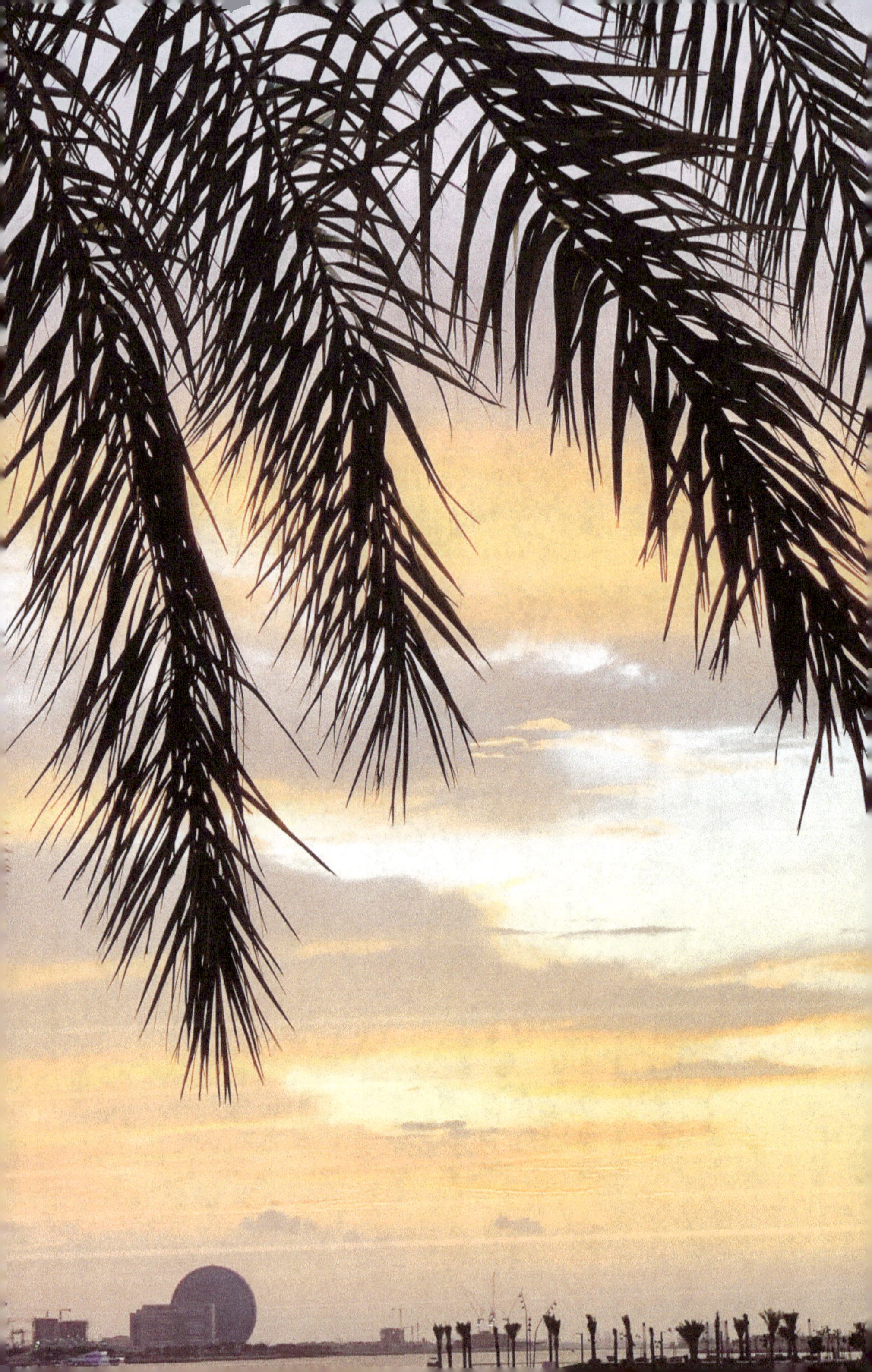

You can hear snippets of conversations in English (with British, Australian, American and other familiar accents), in French, in Russian, in Arabic, and languages I don't recognize. Reminding me of what I love about living in the UAE.

The sea is choppy with the wind blowing it around in different directions. The water lapping against the sea wall sounds soft and calming. Smells of salt, fish and the sea wash over me with every puff of wind. I love the sea. It has been the one constant in my life that grounds me. Boats and water skis move in and out of the channel sometimes gliding quietly and sometimes sounding more like motorcycles on a water freeway. I never grow tired of watching the dance of the water and the things on the water and the sky and the sun.

Today has been another trying day. Since the COVID pandemic started work has become impossible. Every day is a new crisis that I never could have prepared for. Caregivers that are sick, patients that can't get their life-sustaining medications, too many people, not enough people. Each meeting ends in a shouting match with nothing being accomplished and my degree of frustration and disappointment has reached a level even I don't recognize. Instead of spending my down time planning where I will travel next or going to dinner, brunch, happy hour with my friends, tonight I am planning my last trip from the UAE. After months of agonizing, I have reached the painful decision that I need to leave. I need to leave the job because I am not an effective leader anymore. Not my fault really, it's a crisis and times of crisis bring out things no one can predict. If you start with a shaky foundation and you add a crisis, some organizations just can't manage. I have come to realize this is the case and because of the lack of leadership and processes that could lend stability I am growing more and more dissatisfied and less and less productive.

Almost five years ago I arrived in Dubai full of wonder and excitement. A new place, a new start, a new life in every way. I have never lived in a big city filled with so many unique places and people. Now, as I prepare to leave, I am reminded of how special living here was and how big blessings can be! In a funny sort of way, I feel the same wonder and excitement about going home. I don't have a place to live or a job to go to. Life is a little like the water I walk along. Winds blow the water and the water takes the boats, birds, swimmers and fish on a journey that holds something special. I am ready to dive into that water that shines like a million diamonds in the setting sun. Wherever I end up – I know it will be special. Although I won't have my amazing balcony with its sea views and breathtaking sunsets, I will still make my quarantinis and enjoy whatever my new life holds.

MIXOLOGY TIPS

Bar Essentials

Jigger

Mixing spoon

Muddler

Cocktail Shaker

Strainer

Ice tongs

Ice bucket

Use all fresh ingredients if you can – squeeze your own lemon juice, lime juice or orange juice.

Make your own simple syrup. One-part sugar (white or brown) to one-part water. Bring to a boil until all of the sugar is dissolved. Let cool and pour into a small bottle. Keep refrigerated. You can infuse with fresh herbs such as mint or basil. You can also add fresh fruit to the mixture before boiling and then strain through a fine sieve before pouring into the bottle.

Invest in good glassware. A beautiful glass makes even the simplest cocktail taste amazing!

Be generous with the garnish – that's half the fun of the cocktail.

Don't be afraid to experiment. If you don't have one ingredient, substitute something similar that you have on hand.

A well-stocked bar includes: gin, rum, tequila, vodka, whiskey and assorted liqueurs and cordials. You also need to have assorted mixers on hand such as cola, lemon-lime soda, tonic water, ginger ale and juices. Other items that will come in handy are bitters, garnishes, and of course plenty of ice!

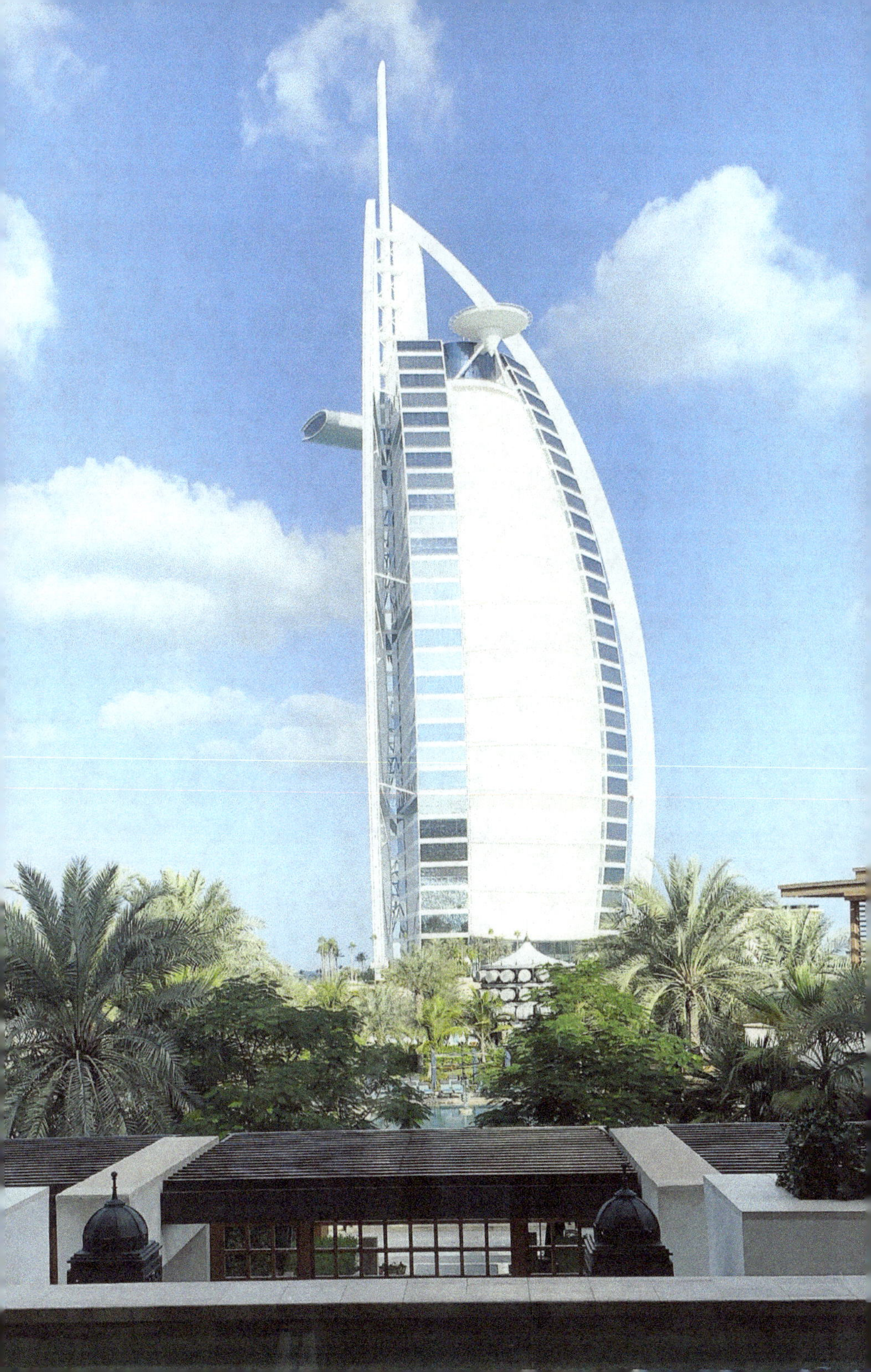

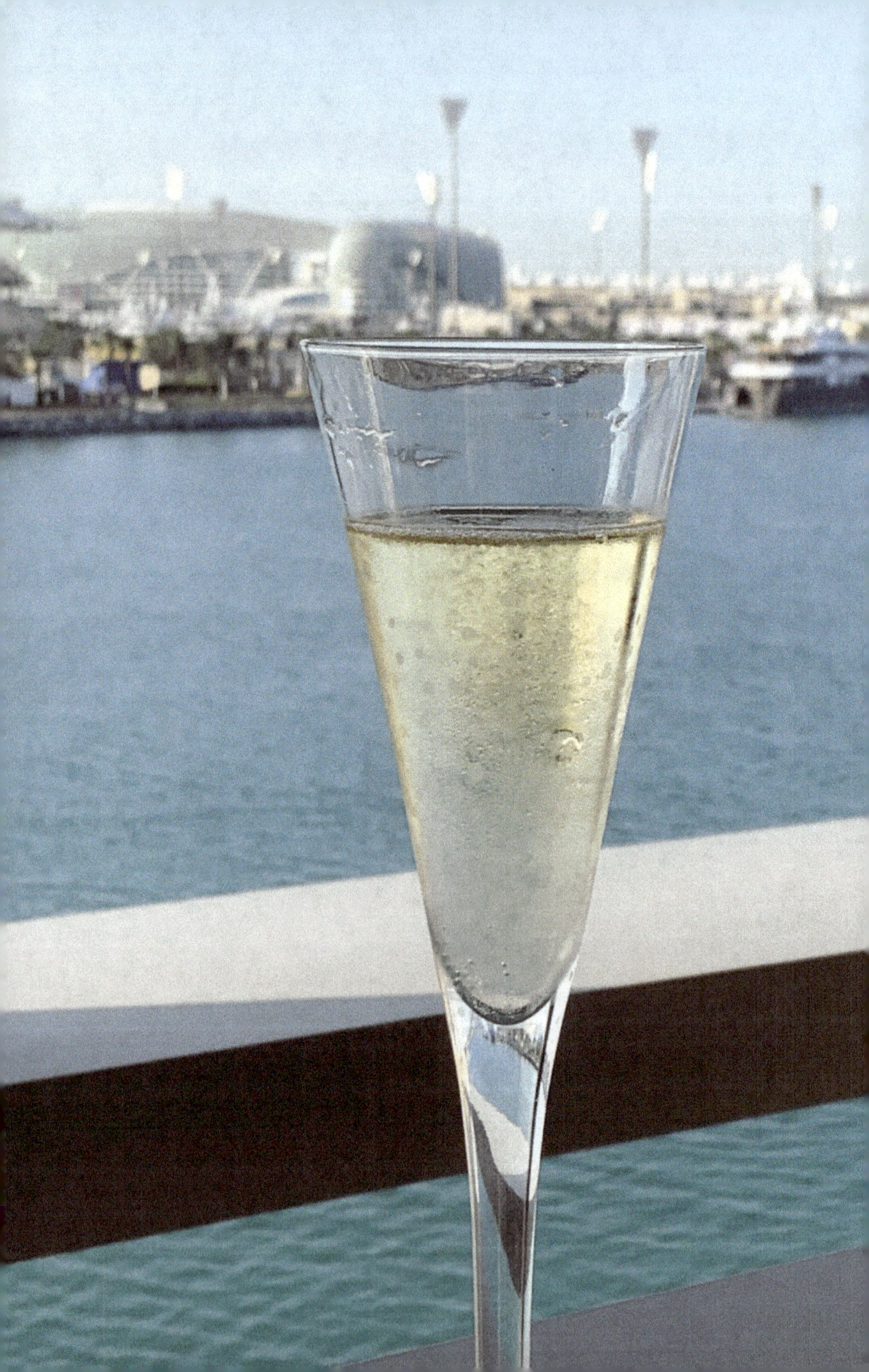

BUBBLES, BLUSH AND BAFOONERY

Some days the level of what we fondly called Bafoonery was just too much to handle. Long, fruitless web meetings that went over the same points in every call were standard fare in the beginning. Confusing and conflicting information from the UAE government and from the world leaders such as Centers for Disease Control and World Health Organization. Panic over lack of personal protective equipment such as masks. On these days, we didn't try to think creatively about the Quarantini of the Day. We simply opened a bottle of bubbles (Veuve Clicquot is my personal favorite) or blush wine (Whispering Angel became our favorite if we could find it) and sat on the balcony watching the water flow to calm our jangled nerves and laughed because we didn't know what else to do!

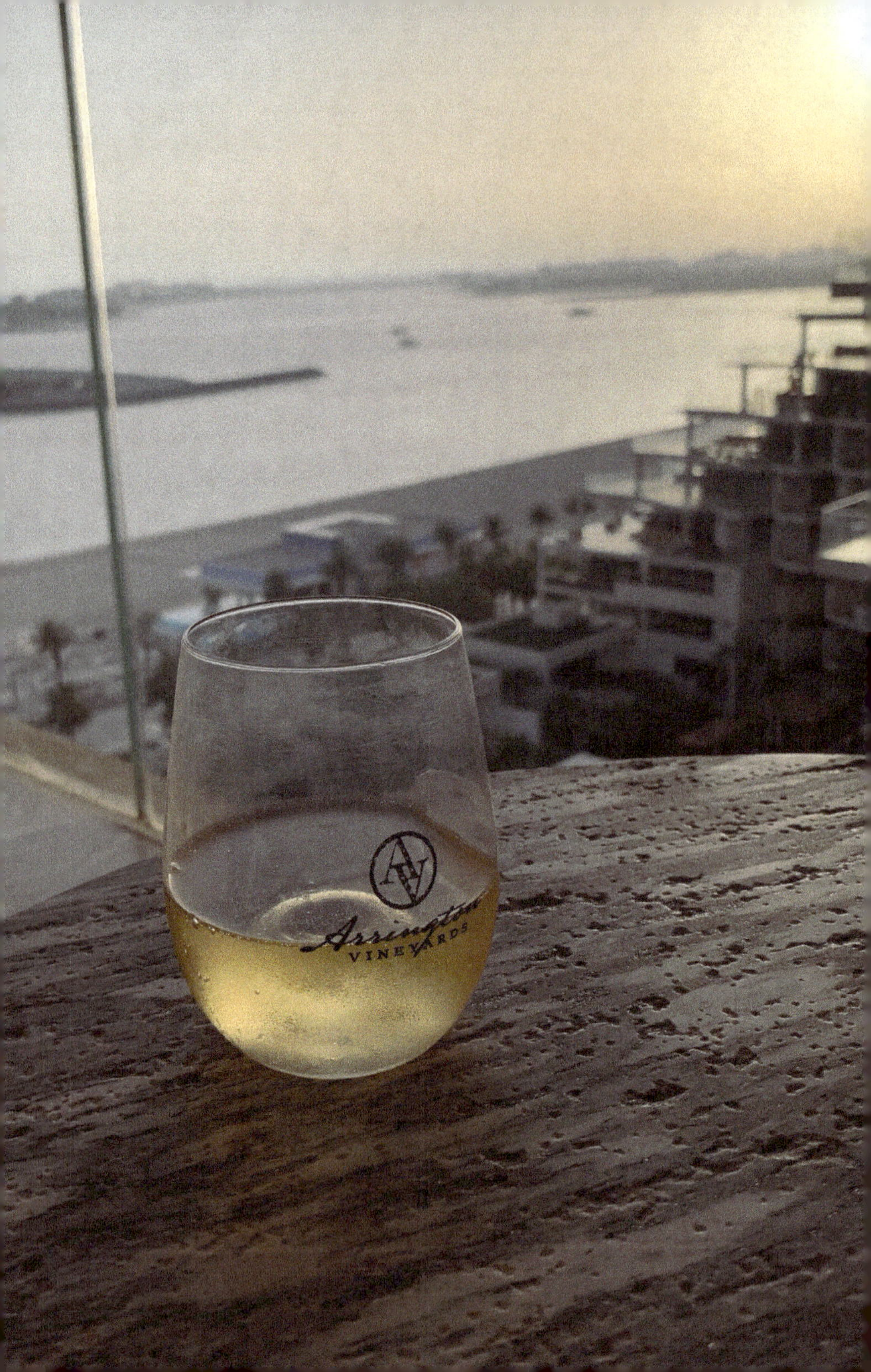

www.ingramcontent.com/pod-product-compliance
Lightning Source LLC
Chambersburg PA
CBHW061441050726
47637CB00002B/8